This is Sweden Calling

**Everything you've ever wanted
to know about the Eurovision
Song Contest but were
laughing too hard to ask!**

DES MANGAN

RANDOM HOUSE AUSTRALIA

Random House Australia Pty Ltd
20 Alfred Street, Milsons Point, NSW 2061
http://www.randomhouse.com.au

Sydney   New York   Toronto
London   Auckland   Johannesburg

First published by Random House Australia 2004

National Library of Australia
Cataloguing-in-Publication Entry

Mangan, Des.
   This is Sweden calling.

   ISBN 1 74051 295 2.

   1. Eurovision Song Contest. 2. Popular music –
   Competitions – Europe. I. Title.

782.42163

Front cover photograph by Richard Bradbury/Getty Images
Back cover photographs and 'Bucks Fizz' photograph by Getty Images
Inside cover photographs by Margaret Meehan
Cover design by Anne Marie Cummins for Uber Creative
Internal design by Anna Warren, Warren Ventures Pty Ltd
Typeset by Midland Typesetters, Maryborough, Victoria
Printed and bound by Griffin Press, Netley, South Australia

10 9 8 7 6 5 4 3 2 1

To Gab.
In my song contest you'll always get
12 points and thank you for reawakening
the child and the passion.

CONTENTS

FOREWORD

by Gina G.

There are about as many books on the Eurovision Song Contest as there are Australians who have competed in the contest. When I first became involved, like most Australians, I had no idea what Eurovision was. For all I knew it could have been a Belgium furniture company.

'Just a Little Bit' wasn't written specifically for Eurovision, but when I performed it at the Great British Song Contest, the preliminary round before the Eurovision Song Contest, and won, my whole world was turned upside down. One minute I had a song which I knew was good, the next minute I would be representing the UK at Eurovision in Norway. Instantly I was on the cover of newspapers and magazines, and appearing on nearly every TV and radio show in the UK, including Top of the Pops which was all I'd ever dreamed of. I suddenly realised I better get serious about this.

Arriving in Norway in May 1996 was a real experience. It was mayhem! Press from every country hovered around us and camped outside our door for interviews and photos. The real eye-opener though was the first sound rehearsal. This was my very first opportunity to see and hear the entries from all the other countries, and what a huge culture shock that was. The first song I heard was the Turkish entry which sounded very strange to me. But that was only the beginning; the rest sounded even stranger – everything from the Irish folk music to the Greek entry. I can tell you, there was a lot of giggling going on backstage!

The biggest question running through my mind was 'What am I doing here?'. 'Just a Little Bit' didn't sound a thing like any one of the other 23 entries. It was a pop song – a thumping 132 beats per minute, 4 on the floor dance track which went straight in at No. 6 in the official UK chart when it was released in March 1996, stayed in the Top 10 week after week and just kept climbing. Eurovision had never before had an entry like that and neither had it seen anything like my girlie dancers or a sparkly dress made of shiny gold discs as short as mine. Still, my aim was to go out there and strut my stuff no matter what the other countries or the panel of fifty-something judges thought.

I'll never forget the feeling of walking out on that stage, 7,000 people to wave at, and I did wave. I knew that 300 million people in Europe were watching from their living rooms. And all I could think about was Mum watching all the way from Australia. My parents

�֍

had never heard of Eurovision either but they thought it was fabulous nonetheless.

Now I have to admit it, I got caught up in all the hype, the glitz and the glamour of it all and by the time all the entries had performed I was desperate to win for the United Kingdom. This lasted all of ten minutes. When the scores started coming in and France gave us 'nul points', I knew we'd lost. I was shocked. Why was it now suddenly political? This is a song contest! We came seventh and the whole of Britain claimed 'we was robbed'. All in all not a bad effort, especially when you look at Britain's 2003 entry, Gemini. No points at all, from anyone!

I think 'Just a Little Bit' made history in a good way. It really did change the face of Eurovision and a lot of countries look for chart success now because they know it's possible. The voting system also changed – since 1996 the public from each country involved is allowed to vote. No more over the hill judges still living in the fifties!

I had a fantastic time and I don't regret a thing. I'm honoured and grateful for the opportunity to represent Britain, now that I know what Eurovision actually is! And you will too by reading this book cover to cover, just a little bit . . . or a little bit more (Ooh Ahh!).

Gina G.

EUROVISION

Qu'est-ce que c'est?

Since its inception in 1956 the Eurovision Song Contest has copped an inordinate amount of flak. Is it compulsory kitsch, a quality contest or colossal crap? Well, basically, it's like religion – it means different things to different people. Since my involvement as commentator for Australian TV station SBS in 2003 I have met a lot of these different people.

There are those who desperately want their country to win and take the whole thing very seriously – to the point of threatening to do something anatomically impossible to me if I so much as offer any criticism about their country's entrant – and there are those who gather together with friends and have huge Eurovision parties, which basically means getting pissed and then taking the piss.

Personally, I love it for all the above reasons. Yes, some of the songs and performances can be gob-smackingly awful and like musical road accidents, you have to slow down to have a look at them. In the same breath, some of the songs and performers can be excellent and, I admit it, I get caught up in the excitement when voting time comes around. I've even been known to be on my feet cheering my favourite entry on. This used to be slightly embarrassing when I watched the telecast on my own but that problem was solved by inviting friends over. I still act like a loony, but it's much easier to explain my behaviour to friends than to inquisitive neighbours who knew that I was home alone.

Too many people try to put the whole contest into one category. They either believe it's all great or it's all garbage. Well, just like life, it's both. That's what makes it great fun. You laugh, you cringe, you cheer, you let yourself get involved. That's where I think a lot of people are missing out on the fun of it – they don't let themselves get caught up in the excitement. It's so easy to be a cynic and say, 'Eurovision? Are you serious? Only geeks watch that.' Well, if that's the case, let me state it clearly: if watching Eurovision makes you a geek, then pass me a live chicken and I'll quite happily bite its head off because I'm a card-carrying, fully paid up member of the Eurovision Geek Club. I love the good songs, the crap ones, the slow ones, the fast ones, the ones that make you tap your feet and the ones that make you want to put your foot through the telly. I love the voting and picking which song I want to win and barracking for it shamelessly. I love the incredibly cheesy banter that every Eurovision host indulges in. I love the fact that Cyprus always give their highest points to Greece and vice versa. I love the fact that France is the only country that won't give their scores in English. I love the fact that most of the Baltic countries only vote for each other. I love it all!

If you can't quite grasp what I'm getting at – that I kind of like the Eurovision Song Contest – then the purpose of this book is, hopefully, to introduce you to the heady joys of all things Eurovision. To that end, let me explain to all you Euro virgins out there just what the whole thing is about.

The Eurovision Song Contest is one of the world's longest running song contests (after the San Remo Song Festival held in Italy) and its aim is simply to unite countries in Europe, on that one night in May, in a friendly contest to find out which has the best (or to be honest, the most popular) song for that year. Although, I must admit, after having been in Latvia for the 2003 event, it ain't always necessarily friendly, but that's behind the scenes. Even at the Oscars, winners get their backs patted onstage only to have them stabbed backstage. It just adds to the catty fun.

Which countries are eligible to compete in the

contest? Basically, any country that is a member of the European Broadcasting Union, who are in charge of the event. The pre-selection rules change almost every year (as I will point out later on) and the number of contestants usually hovers around the 25 mark. Except in 2004, but you'll have to read the rest of the book to find out why that is. So stop standing there flipping through this in the bookshop and cough up the money to buy it. If you have actually bought it, congratulations on your good taste.

Each country that is involved holds a national final earlier in the year to find the song that will represent them. Some countries put on a show that consists of up to 20 singers performing their original songs which are then voted on, either by a jury or by the public. With the advent of reality television, other countries have gone down this path. (Although, the term 'reality television' is really a misnomer as most 'reality' shows bear about as much a resemblance to reality as excrement does to chocolate.) Most recently, Ireland picked their 2003 entrant, Mickey Harte, in a *Popstars*-like TV series called *You're a Star*. (I have a feeling this concept could be picked up by other countries as the guy who owns the format rights was doing his best to flog it to every country involved at the after-show party in Latvia.)

The songs themselves come with a batch of rules. Unlike the Olympics, the contest is not open to just so-called 'amateur' combatants. Any professional performer or songwriter can compete for their country, as was demonstrated by the faux-lesbian Russian duet t.A.T.u. in 2003. The rules state that any song is eligible as long as it hasn't been released or published commercially before the February deadline for the main event. So if there are any budding songwriters out there with a drawer full of unpublished ditties, get over to Sweden, talk a group into doing your song and cross your fingers. But bear in mind the song must not be no longer than 3 minutes duration – if you've written the next 'Bohemian Rhapsody', forget it – and the lyrics of the song must not bring the contest into disrepute, meaning, if your song is called 'The Eurovision Is Complete Shit', you can forget that too.

Usually the host country for the main contest is the country who won the previous year, that is, Turkey won in 2003 so the Eurovision Song Contest 2004 will be held in Istanbul. Much to the delight, I might add, of various commentators I met who have been covering the event for a while and have found themselves in Baltic countries for the past few years. The idea of a warm climate got their little commentator hearts a-flutter.

Sometimes though, with smaller countries, they decline to host even if they do win, usually due to budgetary constraints. Putting on a monumental live event like the Eurovision Song Contest can strain the old pocketbook. In that case another participating country is offered the chance to host.

OK, now we have our winning entries from all the national finals and it has come to the big night. The order the countries perform in has been decided by the drawing of lots in November of the previous year, in the presence of an European Broadcasting Union official, otherwise it would get slightly repetitive if every year Austria started the contest and the United Kingdom finished it. There is also another reason for drawing it this way. Some people claim that the person who goes first is at a bit of a disadvantage because once you have heard about 25 songs you tend to forget the first one. To help counter this, once everyone has performed there is a quick recap of all the songs, starting with the last country first and working backwards. Although by that stage you've either already picked your own personal favourite or the alcohol has kicked in and you can't focus anyway.

Once all the songs have been sung we come to the part of the show that has become a bone of contention with many people over the years – the voting. During an interval in the proceedings, telephone lines throughout Europe open up and everyone has a chance to cast a vote for their favourite performer. Naturally, of course, you can't vote for your own country. If there are any problems with the phones, all countries have a back-up jury of eight people who have been scoring throughout the show and they are then asked for their marks.

When all the voting is done (in the allocated five minutes) a secretary in charge of each country adds up the number of votes – 12 points goes to the song with the most votes, ten points to the second, eight points to the third, seven to the fourth and so on down to one point to the tenth place. This is where the bone of contention comes in. Who gets the points?

For years, critics have cried foul over neighbouring countries voting for each other, but so what? Let's face it, if Australia was involved in a contest with England and New Zealand and there was voting involved, we'd vote for New Zealand. It's not political, it's good old-fashioned rivalry. As long as the Poms don't win, we're happy. Critics, get over it.

A representative from each country appears on the screen announcing who they are (hence the title of this book, *This Is Sweden Calling*) and gives their scores in English or French. Once the scores are all added up, you have a winner. A trophy is handed over to both the singer and the songwriter(s) followed by a reprise of the winning song and it's all over for another year.

Naturally, there's more to Eurovision than this but that's just the basics. Each show usually has two hosts who wear gaudy outfits that would be barred from any Gay Mardi Gras as being too tacky and exchange appalling scripted banter that wasn't even funny when the first caveman slipped on a banana skin.

There's also the interval act, put on by the host country while the voting takes place, which can range from 'what a delightful depiction of local culture' to 'quick, get me a razor blade – I can't take any more of this'.

All of these things combined make Eurovision the great fun that it is.

Now you've had a crash course in Eurovision and how it works, you are primed to enter a musical world where no fashion is too outrageous, no lyric too insane, to learn for yourself why over 600 million televison viewers tune in every year.

Welcome to Eurovision!

THE FIFTIES

From singing 'Refrain' to getting 'A Bit'

In 1955, a film starring Glenn Ford was released called *The Blackboard Jungle*. It was a hard-hitting melodrama about a new teacher starting work at a tough, inner-city New York high school. Apart from having an early appearance by soon-to-be movie star Sidney Poitier, it also had something else – and I'm not just talking about most of the students being played by actors who were older than the teachers. Over the opening credits played a song by the most unlikely of singing sensations: a pudgy, middle-aged rocker called Bill Haley. With his back-up group The Comets, Haley and a little ditty called 'Rock Around The Clock' caused teenage audiences to go ballistic. That event, along with the arrival of a good ol' boy called Elvis (who, ironically, would end up as a pudgy, middle-aged rocker himself) changed popular music as we know it.

Around the the same time over in Monaco, a small committee made up of members of the European Broadcasting Union (EBU) were sitting around trying to think up an idea for a television show that would rally together all the countries in Europe. Of course, these days it'd be easy – they'd just get one contestant from each country, bung them in the same house for three months and hope they shag, but this was the fifties. No, the show they eventually came up with was a song contest that would not influence popular music as we know it one little bit, but it would be bloody good fun.

Before I go any further, just a quick word on the EBU. It was formed on 12 February 1950 by 23 broad-casting organisations from across Europe and the Mediterranean at a conference held in the English coastal resort of Torquay. No word on whether they stayed at Fawlty Towers or not, but I can just imagine the delegate from Spain coming up with a stupid idea (like a song contest) and Basil shaking his head and saying to the rest of the group, 'Please excuse him. He's from Barcelona.'

Out of the EBU came the Eurovision scheme. Put simply, it was a concept whereby the EBU could provide televised news and sporting events to its members at a relatively low cost. Basically, it was one-stop shopping for the smaller countries who may not have had the money or facilities to cover big events; they could simply pay the EBU who would film the event for them and then provide the footage for them to broadcast.

To promote this scheme Marcel Bezençon, the then director-general of Swiss television and a member of the EBU, came up with the idea of a song contest comprising all the member countries. Every-one likes a good sing-a-long, they thought, and so the Eurovision Song Contest was born. Eurovision is much more than just the Song Contest although to this day whenever you mention the word 'Eurovision' to anyone that's what they immediately think of. (Much like many people think Frankenstein is the name of the monster. Not that I'm calling the Song Contest a corpse in desperate need of reanimation. That's the Logies.)

On 19 October 1955 the idea was approved by the EBU General Assembly, held in Rome that year, and it was decided that the first Song Contest would take place on 24 May 1956 in Lugano, Switzerland, the home of the EBU. It was a British journalist who gave it the name Eurovision Grand Prix and even though it still officially bears that title most of us just know it as the Eurovision Song Contest. It's a pity they didn't push that angle. The idea of singers in sequined dresses singing 'La la la la la' as they fanged around a racetrack at 200 kilometres per hour could have been interesting.

Now that they had the idea, the next thing they needed was rules. For the first year, and thankfully only that year, each country was allowed to enter two songs as there were only ten countries participating. If they were allowed to do that now, with more than 24 countries involved, the whole show would go on longer than Gwyneth Paltrow's Oscar acceptance speech.

The EBU recommended that the songs to be entered be picked by each country holding their own national finals and allowing the audience to vote or a selected jury to chose – a practice that remains, with a few exceptions, to this day. There was no rule on what language the song had to be performed in – that was to come later. Juries for the big night were then formed with two delegates from each country awarding from ten points to one point to their favourite songs.

1956

Come the night of the big broadcast, only seven of the ten countries who originally planned to enter performed. They were the Netherlands, Switzerland, Belgium, Germany, France, Luxembourg and Italy. The other three – Denmark, Austria and the United

Kingdom – were disqualified for registering too late. In fact, by the time the United Kingdom finished their national finals, their contestant should have been on stage in Lugano belting out their song. Oops!

Of the 14 songs that were performed, there were some beauties. Some would set the trend for many Euro songs to come. Jetty Paerl from The Netherlands was the first person to sing at Eurovision with her song 'De Vogels Van Holland' ('The Birds of Holland'). With lyrics that go on about Japanese, French and Chinese birds that sing toodledoo, one could be mistaken for thinking it was written by the Monty Python team and, with her constant chirping (exceedingly bad pun intended) about these creatures you'd think she had some sort of bizarre ornithological fetish.

Franca Raimondi's song for Italy called 'Aprite Le Finestre' ('Open The Windows'), while in itself nothing remarkable, was to be groundbreaking in Eurovision terms. Over the years, the contest would garner a reputation for featuring songs with the most banal lyrics imaginable. From 'boom boom' to 'shooby doo' the contest has had them all, but the one that would become a running joke throughout Europe was 'la la la'. How many times could it possibly be used in one song? In her chorus, Franca managed it a grand total of 11 times. This was by no means a Eurovision record (see the 1968 Spanish entry for that dubious honour) but it was the first and that certainly warrants an honourable mention for setting the 'la's' standard.

One of Luxembourg's entries called 'Les Amants de Minuit' ('Midnight Lovers'), sung by Michèle Arnaud, is interesting for its lyrics. It tells the tale of two people and how they met by chance at midnight on the street and there was no pointless talk and no recriminations. Apparently the song is about how love can find you anywhere. Personally, I'm sure it's about hookers.

Other songs of note include one of France's entries, 'Il Est Là' ('He Is There'), sung by Dany Dauberson, relaying that no matter where she looks he is there. Be it in a crowd she sees him or 'just walking down the street – he is there'. This could be the first song ever written about stalking. The Germans had a different way of dealing with love troubles in their song 'So Geht Das Jede Nacht' ('That's How It Is Every Night'). The singer, Freddy Quinn, tells of how his girl goes out with a different bloke every night, so he does one better by going out with a different girl every day. What a remarkably grown-up and mature solution to a relationship in dire need of counselling.

The most depressing song of the contest was definitely the Belgian entry called 'Messieurs Les Noyés De La Seine' ('The Drowned Men Of The River Seine') performed by Fud Leclerc. He drones on about how the girl he loved never loved him and how all his friends have left him, which is no surprise really, considering that he is such a miserable sod. He then goes on to complain that 'I've never known better than love on a stone bed'. Quit your whingeing Fud, wherever you can get it, I always say.

The rest of the entries in the inaugural contest were pretty much songs about lost love, found love or unrequited love. Topics that were to become mainstays in all Eurovision Song Contests, as many of the contest's detractors are quick to point out. They are absolutely right, but have they checked the Top 40 lately?

The big winner was Lys Assia of Switzerland with her song 'Refrain'. Only the winner was announced and the other scores have never been made public. This style of voting was not met with much enthusiasm by the other countries (mainly because they lost). The rule of not being able to vote for your own country was not in force yet, and this, along with Luxembourg not sending a jury and letting the Swiss jury vote for them, did allow the more cynical to cry 'dodgy'.

Even though Switzerland won, they didn't host the 1957 contest. The rule that the winning country hosts the next year's event did not come into practice until 1958.

1957

The second Eurovision Song Contest was held in Frankfurt, Germany, on 3 March 1957. It was agreed at the start that all countries involved would get a chance to host the contest but some say that it's because Germany actually came second in the '56 event that they did the honours. That and maybe they threatened to invade Switzerland.

Naturally, there'd been a few teething problems with the first show so the organisers attempted to iron out the rules and the voting criteria. They didn't. Over the years the rules and the voting would change more times than a bomb disposal expert changes his undies. One rule that was instigated after the 1957 event was the '3 minute rule' stating, obviously, that songs must not exceed 3 minutes in length. This was because of the turgid Italian entry, 'Corde Della Mia Chitarra' ('Strings Of My Guitar'), that dragged on for 5 minutes and 9 seconds. (This may not seem long by today's 'remix' standards, but if you had been forced to sit through it you would have thought of many better uses for the strings of his guitar.)

Speaking of song durations, this year also saw the shortest song ever performed at Eurovision. The English entry 'All', sung by Patricia Bredin, clocked in at 1 minute and 52 seconds. Considering the lyrics of the song read like an obituary – 'All the golden dreams of yesterday . . . All we shared throughout the years' – this was probably a blessing.

Other songs worthy of a mention include the Belgian number sung by Bobbejaan Schoepen, 'Straatdeuntje' ('Street Tune'). Our singer tells of how he keeps hearing a tune in his head as he walks down the street, making it one of the earliest examples of songwriting about mental illness. It's also worth mentioning that he managed to squeeze 13 'tra la's' into the chorus beating the 1956 Italian entry by two 'la's'.

Danièle Dupré's song for Luxembourg, 'Amours Mortes' ('Dead Loves') gave some cause for concern but it had nothing to do with necrophilia, it was just about a girl, heartbroken over a breakup. Damn shame. It certainly would have livened things up a bit. Or deadened them up, as the case may be.

Denmark's performers, Birthe Wilke and Gustav Winckler, also made Eurovision history that night but it had nothing to do with their song 'Skibet Skal Sejle

I Nat' ('The Ship Is Leaving Tonight'). At the end of their performance the two of them were to kiss and a pre-arranged signal was meant to be given to tell them when to stop. The signal never came. It's not known whether a bucket of cold water was poured over the pair but obviously someone eventually intervened, or they might still be love slug wrestling to this day.

The winner on the night, with 31 points, was Corry Brokken from the Netherlands with her song 'Net Als Toen' ('Just Like Then'). A romantic refrain that bemoans the fact that her lover can still flirt even though he is getting fat – an idea that most women will relate to and most men agree with.

To come up with a winner, the voting was changed from the previous year. Ten jury members from each of the ten participating countries gave one point to their favourite song and they were not allowed to vote for their own country. This new voting system would stay in place until 1961, and to keep things on the up and up another great Eurovision mainstay was introduced – the scoreboard.

1958

Nineteen fifty-eight was the first year that the contest was hosted by the previous year's winner – a tradition that continues to this day. On 12 March the third Eurovision was broadcast from Hilversum in the Netherlands and was presented by Hannie Lips. There is no real reason for mentioning her, apart from the fact I just love that name! It should be noted that there was, and is, no set criteria for choosing the comperes. Sometimes they are previous winners, other times they're just popular performers from the host country. Either way, as long as they can read corny jokes off an autocue, they're in with a chance.

This year saw three performers who had previously represented their countries returning for a second shot. Lys Assia, who won the very first Eurovision, was back for Switzerland with a song called 'Giorgio'. Basically, it's about a date with her boyfriend where she drinks numerous bottles of chianti and then sings 'la' 22 times in the chorus. Mind you, if I'd had ten bottles of chianti the only noise I'd be able to make would be 'la'. But this wasn't the 'la' record for 1958. That went to Alice Babs of Sweden with her song 'Lilla Stjärna' ('Little Star'). She managed 36 'la's' in the opening bars alone. In the third year of the event, you can see how the contest was getting a reputation for somewhat simplistic lyrics.

Another returnee for that year was Fud Leclerc of Belgium with a song entitled 'Ma Petite Chatte' ('My Little Sweetie'). A dubious song where he sings about his sweetie who looks 'a bit strange' and looks 'a bit bad' and all she has to do is 'pleasure boys'. I hate to be the one to tell you this Fud, but your little sweetie ain't that sweet.

Corry Brokken, the previous year's winner, came back with a song called 'Heel De Wereld' ('The Whole World') in which she spends the whole song telling us that she has a secret only to reveal . . . she's happy. A bit anti-climactic. Now, if she had told us who shot Kennedy, *that* would have been a secret worth revealing.

The winner for that year with 27 points was France with their entry 'Dors, Mon Amour' ('Sleep, My Love'), by André Claveau, but the most interesting song of the year was the Italian entry, 'Nel Blu Dipinto Di Blu' (In The Blue Painted In Blue) sung by Domenico Modugno. On the night, due to technical problems, some of the countries watching did not pick up his performance. To be fair, the organisers waited until all the songs had finished and let him perform it again. Although he only managed to come in third, there was an upside to this. His song was picked up by an American performer and became a huge hit. The performer was Dean Martin and the song became known as 'Volare'. It went on to win two Grammy Awards possibly making it the most well-known song that never won Eurovision.

1959

This year Eurovision moved on to Cannes, France. On 11 March, 11 countries took to the stage. One of the odder entries would have to be the Austrian contestant, Ferry Graf, and his song 'Der K Und K Kalypso Aus Wien' ('The K And K Calypso From Vienna'). Vienna and calypso are not usually two things that are musically linked. It'd be like Hawaiian hip hop. The rest of the world wasn't impressed either as poor old Ferry came in equal second last with 4 points.

It should be noted that this wasn't the first odd song to come from Austria. Nineteen fifty-seven saw Bob Martin sing a strange little number called 'Wohin, Kleines Pony?' ('Where, Little Pony?') and they have kept this tradition going, right up to the eccentric performance of Alf Poier in 2003 (more on him later). Go, the Austrians!

Birthe Wilke was back for Denmark (no tonsil hockey this time – she sang solo) with her entry called 'Uh – Jeg Ville Ønske Jeg Var Dig' ('Oh, I Wish I Were You') where she hit a new high in lyrics, even for Eurovision. This time she went one up from the usual 'la's' and went for the 'da doo da da dey da doo's' instead. A woman ahead of her time. The song also says 'if I were you I'd go kiss myself'. Change one word and you could use this song if you're ever in an argument with someone.

Although it wasn't a very eventful year, in the history of Eurovision, there was some controversy. The night was won by the Netherlands and Teddy Scholten with her song 'Een Beetje' ('A Bit') which sounds like it could have been sung by Benny Hill or any of the Carry On team. But no, that wasn't the controversial bit. The controversy came the next day when the press suggested that Italy and France gave so many points to the Netherlands because the two countries didn't want each other to win. This wouldn't be the last time the politics of voting was called into question.

If you were asked to pick a decade that had a defining effect on popular music, you would have to choose the fifties. From the safety of Frank Sinatra and big bands came the supposed threat of Elvis and rock'n'roll. Things were never going to be the same.

However, mainstream television didn't immediately embrace the new sound; stations were more concerned with the family audience. Their variety shows had men in tuxedos and women in sensible long dresses with hairstyles that defied gravity, singing songs that would not encourage youngsters to indulge in wanton acts of carnality. This was what the Eurovision Song Contest was like in the fifties: a time delayed reflection of the cultural change that was sweeping across the world.

After just four years, the contest had become incredibly popular but that was nothing compared to the dizzy heights it would reach in the psychedelic sixties when things changed and performers would sing – shock, shock, horror, horror – barefooted!

THE SIXTIES

Starts with just 'Tom' but ends in a foursome

B y the time the sixties rolled around the Euro-vision Song Contest was firmly ensconced as a television favourite. The number of participating countries had risen to 13 as more and more countries joined the EBU. Finland decided to broadcast the contest live for the first time and things were generally looking good, but this was the decade that would experience the biggest controversy in Eurovision history.

1960

Even though the Netherlands won in 1959 they didn't want to be the first host of the new decade. They had already won twice and felt that hosting it again in such a short space of time wasn't a good idea. The honour then fell to the United Kingdom and on 25 March the fifth Eurovision Song Contest went to air.

Being the host country the British were naturally hoping they'd do well and their entry by Bryan Johnson (no, not the lead singer of AC/DC, more's the pity) called 'Looking High, High, High' was a hot contender. Unfortunately, poor old Bryan looked pretty straight, straight, straight and he only managed second place.

The previous year's winner, the Netherlands, came up with a song performed by Rudi Carrell called 'Wat Een Geluk'('What Luck') telling us he was so happy that there are daffodils, butterflies, birds, fish and fruit in the world. Forget the British entry, I think this was the guy who was high, high, high.

Denmark's entrant was Katy Bødtger with her song 'Det Var En Yndig Tid' ('It Was A Lovely Time'). A nostalgic ode that talked about a time when things were better: when girls would ask their mothers if they could go out and they would go courting wearing crinolines. There's something about the way this song pines for yesteryear that reminds me of the old guy on the bus who whinges about how things were better in his day and what the young people of today need is a 'good World War – that'll sort them out'. One day I hope somebody writes a song called 'Things Were Crap Back Then: I Much Prefer It Now'. Future Eurovision lyricists take note.

Fud Leclerc from Belgium declared his love in 'Mon Amour Pour Toi' ('My Love For You'), a moving tune where he lists the things he would share with his true love, including ice water and bread. I'm not sure if he was trying to tell his beloved he's a cheap date or that he's actually in prison.

A relatively uneventful year, song-wise and rule changing-wise, the winner was France with 32 points for their song 'Tom Pillibi' performed by Jacqueline Boyer. The song was a fairytale about a guy who has two castles, two ships and is apparently evil, but our singer still loves him. Goes to show things haven't changed much – even back then women were still going for bastards with money. (A note for Eurovision trivia buffs: Jacqueline was the daughter of Jacques Pills, who performed for Monaco the previous year. Poor old dad came last in his attempt. I wonder if it's ever mentioned around the family dinner table?)

1961

Nineteen sixty-one saw the contest back in France and the number of participating countries jumped to 16. Finland sent an entry for the first time, starting an incredible record in Eurovision to date. So far, they hold the record for being the country that has participated in the most Eurovision Song Contests without ever winning – a grand total of 37 times in all. They don't, however, hold the record for getting the most 'nul points' in Eurovision. That goes to Norway with a record breaking four times. Not something to brag about but, hey, it's something!

Special note should be made of the trend that started of doing weather reports in the songs. Norway's 'Sommer I Palma' ('Summer in Palma') and Sweden's 'April, April' both extolled the virtues of sunshine on a relationship. Although Belgian Bob Benny's attempt to blame the break-up of his relationship on the cold weather in his song 'Septembre, Gouden Roos' ('September, Golden Rose') seemed to be clutching at straws. You think I'm kidding about this? Monaco's entry by Collette Deréal called 'Allons, Allons Les Enfants' ('Let's Go, Let's Go Children') sang about the first day of spring. In Spain's song 'Estando Contigo' ('Being With You'), Conchita Bautista tells us that she's so in love she doesn't notice when it's snowing and Lale Andersen from Germany in 'Einmal Sehen Wir Uns Wieder' ('We'll Meet Again') reports that Sunday was grey and the rain hammered down. I'm telling you, there were no singers that year, only meteorologists.

Just as an aside, although the Swedish song 'April, April' was sung on the night by Lill-Babs, she didn't actually perform it at the Swedish national finals. It was sung by former Eurovision contestant Siw Malmkvist but she couldn't stop laughing so she was replaced. Considering the lyrics talk about how happy the boys are that the girls have changed their woollen socks to nylon ones and 'all the lively happy birds are singing chirp, chirp, chirp', I don't blame her. I would have been on the floor myself.

The winner for that year was Jean-Claude Pascal from Luxembourg with his song 'Nous Les Amoureux' ('We The Lovers'), but I think a special award should have gone to the songwriters of the Danish entry, 'Angelique', sung by Dario Campeotto. Any lyricist who comes up with the idea of rhyming 'violin' with 'Menuhin' (a famous musician) deserves some prize, surely.

1962

It's time to change the voting again! This time the ten members from each country's national jury gave three points to their favourite song, two points to their second favourite and one to their third. All added up, this came to 60 points awarded by each country. Then they looked at which three songs got the most points and the top three were given three, two and one points respectively and these were plastered onto the Eurovision scoreboard. Confusing? Everyone else thought so too because this only lasted for one more year before it all changed again in 1964.

Doing the voting this way meant it was possible for some countries to get 'nul points' (nil points). For the first time ever, four countries – Belgium, Spain, Austria and the Netherlands – got the big zero. All this was obviously too much for Belgian contestant Fud Leclerc, who had participated a few times in Eurovision, because he never entered again. Which is a damn shame. Anyone who has a name that makes them sound like the villain in a bad sixties spy movie is a definite must for Eurovision.

Looking at the other songs that received 'nul points', it's not hard to see why. The Austrian entry by Eleonore Schwarz called 'Nur In Der Wiener Luft' ('Only In The Air In Vienna') asked the question, 'Can you smell a waltz?'. Apparently in Vienna you can. The Netherlands' song 'Katinka' by De Spelbrekers included more 'la la's' and told of two sleazy blokes who, every morning at 8.30, watch a girl out walking with her mum (lock them up – NOW!) and the

Spanish 'Llamame' ('Call Me') was also full of 'la la's'
– 15 in all.

One thing this new voting did show was a definitive
winner as France bolted home with a clear 26 points
for Isabelle Aubret and her song 'Un Premier Amour'
('A Great Love').

Most importantly, the United Kingdom's Ronnie
Carroll kept up the Eurovision tradition of meaningful
lyrics with his song 'Ring-a-Ding Girl' in which he
managed to get the word 'ding' into the song an
outstanding 113 times. Surely he deserved something
for that. A kick in the bells, at least. The only other
song of interest that year was Sweden's entry called
'Sol Och Vår' ('Sun and Spring') in which a woman
offers to help a man chose a ring for his fiancée.
He offers to buy her lunch and then proceeds to bugger
off from the restaurant with her fur coat.

1963

Even though France had won the previous year, just
like the Netherlands in 1960 they decided not to host
the '63 contest because they had done so just two years
before. When a winning country decides not to host,
the job is frequently offered to one of the bigger-paying

members of the EBU so it was off to England. And, surprise, surprise, there was a change in the voting system! This time the number of jury members for each country was increased to 20 and they were allowed to vote for their top five songs giving them five, four, three, two and one points, respectively. It was getting to the stage where you needed a scorecard to keep track of things. (Don't get too used to it though, things would change again the next year.)

Ronnie 'Ring-a-Ding' Carroll was the United Kingdom's entry for a second year with his song 'Say Wonderful Things' expressing how he wants a girl to say wonderful things to him. Nowadays, there are special phone numbers for that sort of thing. José Guardiola performed for Spain with 'Algo Prodigioso' ('Something Marvellous'), which, obviously, it wasn't because it came twelfth, Finland's song 'Muistojeni Laulu' ('Song Of My Memories') sung by Laila Halme contained a mammoth 36 'la la's' in the opening verse. Or maybe it didn't. Maybe poor Laila just forgot the words on the night. Perhaps this is the reason that there are so many 'la la's' in Eurovision songs. Stage fright.

Yet again it was a year of falling in and out of love and singing about the icy weather. It seems that to write a surefire winner for Eurovision all you have to do is fall in love, walk in the rain and sing 'la la' a couple of hundred times. (If anyone out there tries this formula and wins, I expect royalties.)

The German entrant, Heidi Brül, in her song 'Marcel' wished the title character could be nicer because 'only a gentleman has a chance with me'. Yet she neglects to mention just exactly what he's doing that makes him so awful. I look forward to a Eurovision song where a woman sings of her loved one playing Dutch Ovens or biting his toenails off and keeping the clippings in an ashtray.

Love was also on the mind of the Yugoslavian singer Vice Vukov, but not his love for someone or someone's love for him. In his song 'Brodovi' ('Ships'), Vice tells us that in his neighbourhood 'ships are like people, they cry, smile and love'. Either this is a simile too clever for me to grasp or Vice is clinically insane.

Monica Zetterlund from Sweden tells us in her song 'En Gång I Stockholm' ('Once Upon A Time In Stockholm') that 'the bells of the German church, silently call "ding dong"'. Just one question, Monica. If the bells are silent, how can you hear the 'ding dong'? They could be calling 'sing song', 'King Kong' or 'bong on', for that matter.

The ultimate winner was Denmark with the song 'Dansevise' ('Dance Ballad') performed by Grethe and

Jørgen Ingmann. This song consists, naturally, of lots of sunshine and wind and unrequited love.

1964

Grethe and Jørgen's win saw the 1964 Eurovision take place in Copenhagen and 'nul points' for guessing what happened. That's right – a change in the voting system. To simplify it, and to stop this whole book reading like an accountant's ledger, after going through a long, drawn-out process each country awarded five, three and one point to its top three songs.

This year saw the first political protester interrupt the broadcast as he jumped on stage holding a banner that read 'Boycott Franco and Salazar'. The broadcasters didn't want politics to get in the way of the contest (that only happens in the voting) so a shot of the scoreboard was shown until the man was removed from the stage.

The show continued with some of Eurovision's stranger songs making an appearance, including Spain's entry Los TNT – otherwise known as Tim, Nelly and Tony – singing about their hearts becoming 'your conch of love', and Arne Bendiksen from Norway who, in the middle of his song 'Spiral', just sang 'bong' and then went on to say his life had taken shape under a pink balloon. This could explain the 'bong'.

Austria's performer Udo Jürgens with his song 'Warum Nur Warum?' ('Why Only Why?') proceeded to moan about 'why did you go and why do flowers die?'. Not to be outdone, Germany's entry by Nora Nova called 'Mann Gewöhnt Sich So Schnell An Das Schöne' (which, for trivia buffs, is the longest Eurovision song title ever and translated means 'How Quickly We Get Used To The Nice Things') bleated on about how, eventually, all relationships end and what a disappointment that is. These two cheery buggers are the sort of people I usually get stuck next to in the pub.

Anneke Grönloh from the Netherlands gave us the haunting 'Jij Bent Mijn Leven' ('You Are My Life') in which she says 'I know that you're lying and that you're cheating but I accept it'. She should have changed the name of the song from 'You Are My Life' to 'I Am A Doormat'. Speaking of people wanting to be inanimate objects, in his song 'Život Je Sklopio Krug' ('Life Has Completed The Circle') Sabahudin Kurt from Yugoslavia sings that if he became a branch his 'leaves would ponder'. I think the branch analogy is quite appropriate here as the man is obviously out of his tree.

Britain's entry that year was 'I Love The Little Things' by Matt Monro, a performer who appeared on the famous goon, Peter Sellers' album, 'Songs for Swingin' Sellers', and sang the theme song for the Bond film *From Russia With Love*. But even with all this behind him he only managed to come in second with 17 points. The resounding winner was Gigliola Cinquetti from Italy who scored a whopping 49 points with 'Non Ho L'Étà' ('I'm Too Young') – a love song that could open the floodgates for a spate of jokes but I'll let good taste prevail.

1965

Naples, Italy and the first signs of a feminist attitude were creeping into the songs. Conny van den Bos with her song for the Netherlands called 'Het Is Genoeg' ('It's Enough') explains how all men lie and cheat and that she's had enough. Birgit Brüel for Denmark with 'For Din Skyld' ('For Your Sake') tells her man that she wasn't his prey but his peer. You go, girls. Sadly, they were let down by the Belgian performer Lize Marke and her song 'Als Het Weer Lente Is' ('When It's Springtime Again' – more bloody weather!) where she carries on like a total subservient, doing everything for her man. She closes the doors, turns off the lights – the woman's not a lover, she's a friggin' caretaker!

Poor Spain didn't fare too well with 'Qué Bueno, Qué Bueno' ('How Good, How Good') in which Conchita Bautista repeated the phrase 'how good, how good' 40 times in under 3 minutes. Clearly, she wasn't that good as the song received 'nul points' – not good, not good.

This was also the year that the Soviet Union picked up the broadcast and Ireland entered the contest for the first time, coming sixth with Butch Moore's song 'I'm Walking The Streets In The Rain'. After a slow start, Ireland would soon become a force to be reckoned with, going on to win the contest a record-breaking seven times.

Germany's Ulla Wiesner gave us another tale of lost love with 'Paradies, Wo Bist Du?' ('Paradise, Where Are You?') in which she sings 'first a look . . . then a kiss . . . then the day . . . then the light'. Whoa, Ulla, you left out the good stuff. What happened between the kiss and the day? Admittedly, with censorship being what it was on television in the sixties, 'then a shag, then a fag' probably wouldn't have been acceptable. Not necessarily though, when you look at Norway's entry, 'Karusell' ('Merry-Go-Round') sung by Kirsti Sparboe. In it she talks about how she likes two blokes,

Kjell and Arne, and how they are both taking her out that day. But her dilemma is which one to be with. Eventually, she picks Kjell and says 'he can take me home. Poor Arne must stand there and watch'. Kinky. Maybe sixties telly was a bit more permissive than I've been led to believe.

Luxembourg walked away with the Grand Prix of Eurovision with their song 'Poupée De Cire, Poupée De Son' ('Doll Of Wax, Doll Of Sound') performed by the lovely France Gall, who likens her head to a record album. No, not black and circular with a hole in the middle but full of music and sound. It's probably the weirdest title of a Eurovision-winning song, and that in itself is no small feat.

1966

Luxembourg was the next host and was witness to a major change in the rules. Possibly because the 1965 Swedish entry 'Absent Friend' by Ingvar Wixell had been sung in English, it was decreed that from now on songs could only be sung in one of the country's national languages (but, of course, like all things Eurovision, that would change later).

It wouldn't be a Eurovision without at least one

goofy song and this year's winner (although it wasn't the official winner, but it is in my books!) was Sweden's 'Nygammal Vals' ('New-Old Waltz') which also had the extra title of 'Hip Pig Breeder'. The song was a fairytale about a pig breeder and a princess who decide to swap places. He goes to the palace and she bangs his saucepan. The moral being, as they state in the song, that trading your saucepan can be a bad idea. The thing that makes this song so kitsch is they try to modernise the fable – well, sixties modern anyway – by using terms like 'really happening', 'groovy tune', 'I'm hip' and 'you dig'. Mind you, it's not that out of date and it just proves that everything is cyclical as kids are now using terms like 'cool' and 'chill out' in this new millennium. I'm just showing my age by remembering the terms the first time around.

Spain, inspired by France's 1956 entry, had Raphael sing a stalking song called 'Yo Soy Aquel' ('I'm That One'). In it, our Spanish serenader reveals that he's the one who 'chases you every night and who waits for you'. The next line should have been 'I'm the one you should take out a restraining order against'. Finland took a swipe at this macho posturing with 'Playboy' sung by Ann-Christine Nyström in which she goes on about how the playboy of the title likes to think he is 007 but 'forget the seven, you're just a zero'. Ouch!

Another blow to the male ego came from the Danish entry 'Stop, Mens Legen Er Go' ('Stop, While The Going Is Good') performed by Ulla Pia. The song tells the tale of a girl who is walking home from her first dance. When the boy makes a pass at her she sings, 'stop, while the going is good. Let's just aimlessly wander on. Enjoy the tranquillity of the starry sky, it was made for us'. Nicely put. It's certainly much better than the soul-destroying, 'I just love you like a friend' or the potential physical danger of, 'try that again and I'll knee you in the balls'.

After his third year in a row performing for Austria, Udo Jürgens finally won for his homeland with the song 'Merci Chérie' ('Thank You, Darling'). I'm sure that after trying for so long poor old Udo certainly was flippin' thankful.

1967

Nineteen sixty-seven saw the contest held in Austria and, of course, with a new year came – you guessed it – a change in the voting. For some strange reason, the EBU decided to revert back to the way the voting had been done in 1957 (ten jury members from each country giving one point to their favourite song and they couldn't vote for their own country), positive that this time it would work. This was going to be the definitive voting system for the Eurovision Song Contest. No changes. This was it! . . . Well, until 1970 anyway.

This Eurovision was a benchmark year for your author. This was the year that, as a five-year-old, I not only got drunk for the first time (but that's another story), but I saw my first Eurovision Song Contest. There I was, huddled up in front of the telly in my pyjamas in our little house in Daffodil Street, East Acton, in London, getting extremely excited as I watched a bare-footed Sandie Shaw win it for England with 'Puppet On A String'. To this day, I can still sing all the words to that song. (God help you if it's on a karaoke machine and I've got enough beers under my belt. I warn you, I will kill to get the microphone.)

While I'm reminiscing (that is, being self-indulgent), another of this year's songs brought back something else from my childhood. The song was 'O Vento Mudou' ('The Wind Has Changed') by Eduardo Nascimento from Portugal. Basically, he sings about a girl who's dumped him because she promised to return when the wind changed but she didn't. It's the title of the song that reminds me of my younger days. I don't know about you, but when I was a kid if I was ever being obnoxious and pulled a funny face, my mum would always say, 'You know, if the wind changes, your face will stay like that'. Even now, if I'm walking down the street and I see someone blood-freezingly ugly, I always think to myself, 'Whoa, the wind obviously changed when they were pulling that one'. Maybe Eduardo should have gone with my version as he only managed twelfth place.

Right, self-indulgent ramble over, back to the lovely Sandie, bringing it home for England. Up until this point, the United Kingdom had never won the contest but they had come in second place five times in the previous nine years, and Sandie was certainly up against some stiff competition – hers wasn't the only song about puppets that year. The entry from Norway, 'Dukkemann' ('Puppet Man') sung by Kirsti Sparboe reminded us that 'we must understand, that we must jump like everyone on a string'. I don't know what they were taking in Norway but I wish they'd pass some around to the rest of us.

Depression also seemed to be a bit of a theme at this year's event with Louis Neefs from Belgium in his song 'Ik Heb Zorgen' ('I Have Worries') singing 'I have worries and that bores me a lot'. Not half as much as you bored us, Louis. The Netherlands kept the cheer going with their little number, 'Ring-Dinge-Ding'

('Ring-Ding-A-Ding'), in which their singer, one Thérèse Steinmetz, tells us that she feels like drinking vodka in the morning. These morning libations could definitely help explain why she sang 'ring-ding-a-ding' 25 times in the chorus.

On an up note for Eurovision, this year introduced something that has since become an integral part of the Eurovision Song Contest broadcast. For the first time, there were cameras in the green room and shots were beamed out of the artists and their entourages sitting at tables waving their country's flag, pretending to smile when another country got more points.

1968

With England's win the whole show moved to the Royal Albert Hall and to something that the Eurovision Song Contest had been crying out for – for the first time it was broadcast in colour. All those sequins and plush purple velour suits could now be seen the way they were meant to be seen – in glorious, eye-straining colour. This was something that the United Kingdom's entry took full advantage of. Performing his song 'Congratulations', well-known tennis fan and professional virgin Cliff Richard appeared in an incredible blue velvet number, set off by a ruffled white shirt – an outfit that may have been groovy at the time (though I doubt it), in retrospect it makes him look like Austin Powers.

The garish outfit didn't help much and poor old Cliff came in second with 28 points. Although, it was right down to the wire, the winner Massiel from Spain just pipped him at the post with 29 points with his song 'La, La, La'. Britain did complain that Spain had deliberately not voted for Cliff in order to make England lose, but the complaint about Spain fell mainly down the drain and they remained the winners. In a double victory, Spain also managed to break the 'la la' record, their song containing 138 'la's' – a definite winner. Still the record holder today, the closest contender yet was the 1982 Irish entry 'Here Today, Gone Tomorrow', which contained 111 'la's'.

The Spaniards were also embroiled in political Eurovision problems before they even arrived at the Albert Hall. Their song was originally supposed to have been sung by Juan Manuel Serrat but as he would only sing in Catalan, forbidden at that time by the Franco regime, he was replaced by Massiel. Juan could have stood his ground against the dictator but who wants 'Shot For Going To The Eurovision Song Contest' written on their gravestone?

One of the things I really love about the lyrics of a Eurovision song is that they can usually find a very flowery and verbose way of saying something that's quite simple. Case in point, this year's Belgian entry, 'Quand Tu Reviendras' ('When Will You Come Back') by Claude Lombard (that's a she, by the way). Rather than just saying 'I really hope you come back', she warbles 'I'm turning incessantly my spinning wheel of hope'. Same goes for the Austrian entry Karel Gott (that's a he, by the way) in his song 'Tausend Fenster' ('Thousands Of Windows') who can't just say 'it's night-time' but has to say 'now the city wears an evening dress'. I don't know which city he's talking about but I can only assume it's either Sydney or San Francisco.

Other songs included another downer of an entry from the Netherlands, 'Morgen' ('Morning'), with the singer Ronnie Tober referring to mornings as being a sad fare and a cliché. Something I can totally sympathise with, Ronnie, because I'm not a morning person either. Claes-Göran Hederström from Sweden sang 'Det Börjar Verka Kärlek Banne Mej' ('It's Beginning To Look Like Love, Damn It') about how, with his new girlfriend, he no longer goes to see action movies but instead sees girlie ones, and how he no longer goes out with his mates but goes to visit his girlfriend's mother. I'm afraid it's not beginning to look like love, Hederström, it's beginning to look like you're a big wuss.

One of the oddest entries to date made its appearance at this contest. I use the term odd intentionally as the singer's name is Odd Børre, and the song was Norway's entry, called 'Stress'. Our Odd friend sang about the things that stress him out. The biggest one of all was stressing about catching the last bus home. He goes on (and on and on) about how he 'must, must, must, must, must, hurry up and go, go, go, go'. For all this anxiety he advocates tea with lemon and 'sleeping pills in small doses', of course. If he's still performing today, I can recommend a song title for him – 'Prozac Is My Friend'.

1969

Spain's win meant the 1969 Song Contest took place in Madrid but since Franco was still ruling, Austria bowed out, refusing to send an entrant to a country run by a dictator. It was also an interesting year for the fact that noted surrealist artist Salvador Dali created all the publicity artwork. But these weren't the main factors that made 1969 a notable year in Eurovision Song Contest history.

For the first time ever, there was a four-way tie for first place: Spain with their song 'Viva Cantando' ('Long Live Singing') by Salomé, the Netherlands with 'De Troubadour' ('The Troubadour') by Lenny Kuhr, France with 'Un Jour, Un Enfant' ('A Day, A Child') by Frida Boccara and the United Kingdom with 'Boom Bang A Bang' by Lulu (who should've gone to a cardiologist immediately as she constantly complained about her heart going 'boom bang a bang' – never a good sign).

Hard as it is to believe, there were no solutions in the rules for this situation so they were all declared winners and given medals. Actually, since medals are usually awarded to the singer and the songwriters, they didn't have enough to go around on the night so the songwriters had to wait until later to get theirs. This is the sort of thing I'd love to see at the Oscars: 'Um, look, sorry about this, Russell, but we've run out of statues. Tell you what. You're bound to get nominated again next year, we'll give you two then.'

Historically, the sixties were a turbulent time, with the assassinations of the Kennedys and Martin Luther King, the Vietnam War and protests around the world. Musically, it was also a time of change, from the early pop songs of the Beatles to their change of direction in the latter part of the decade, to the protest songs of

Bob Dylan and the Woodstock phenomenon. Things weren't exactly quiet in Europe either, with the building of the Berlin Wall, the Pope changeover and the dictatorship in Spain. But did the Eurovision Song Contest reflect any of these major cultural and political events? You bet your sweet 'la-la's' they didn't, not one 'boom bang a bang' bit. The contest was there to provide viewers with an escape from all this turmoil, but it was going to need to do something to prove itself as a major musical force.

To show that the contest had credibility and musical relevance, it needed to produce a winner that would go on to unprecedented international success and, in the seventies, it would do just that.

THE SEVENTIES

From shamrock to shalom

1970

After the voting debacle of the 1969 contest, the first thing that needed to be worked out was where the 1970 Eurovision Song Contest was actually going to be held. Lots were drawn by the four winning countries and the Netherlands won. Eurovision was off to Amsterdam.

To make sure the same four-way-tie disaster didn't happen again, the voting system was changed. Bet you didn't see that coming. This time, if there was a draw, the tied contestants would have to perform their songs again and the juries of the other competing countries (who were present at the event) would vote by a show of hands. If the contestants were tied again after this round of voting then multiple winners would be declared. This time, the EBU thought, they had it. It was foolproof. No need to change this voting procedure . . . well, until the next year anyway.

However, it seemed these changes weren't acceptable to some countries, who were still mightily miffed at the previous year's outcome, so Portugal, Finland, Norway and Sweden boycotted the event, bringing the number of participating countries down to 12.

With all this going on, there was a little uncertainty as to whether the Eurovision Song Contest had any kind of future but the Dutch plodded on regardless, although they must have thought it was some kind of omen when the stage collapsed during the dress rehearsal.

For the start of the new decade, there was a pretty mixed bag of songs. The Belgian singer Jean Vallée gave a rendition of 'Viens L'Oublier' ('Try To Forget Him') in which he tells a woman that the lover she had was no good for her because he only made her suffer. In other words, he's a bastard – I'm not. Nice try, Jean. It's right up there with 'I'm in touch with my feminine side' as one of the worst ploys in trying to get a woman into bed.

Yugosalvia went with the woman's point of view as Eva Sršen in 'Pridi, Dala Ti Bom Cvet' ('Come, I'll Give You The Flower') sang about the flower that grows inside her. As with Lulu in 1969, I would suggest immediate medical attention for a condition like this.

Monaco took an entirely different tack, singing about a famous movie star. Dominique Dussault sang

'Marlene', a tribute to the famous German actress Marlene Dietrich, describing her as 'a silhouette in sexyrama' – a film process I haven't heard about. She adds to this that Marlene was one-metre-fifty in heels and had hair like a sheep. Sure you're not thinking about Harpo, Dominique?

Two acts that year who were to receive international recognition were the United Kingdom's Mary Hopkin and Spain's Julio Iglesias. Hopkin sang 'Knock Knock (Who's There?)' – a joke she never finished, by the way. The song became a worldwide hit for her, along with 'Those Were The Days'. Inglesias sang 'Gwendolyne' and despite coming equal fourth went on to international success. Special note should be made of his light, sea-blue suit and tie, worn with an even lighter blue shirt. If he had added blue make-up he could easily have passed as a Spanish Smurf.

But the night really belonged to Ireland, who won with Dana singing 'All Kinds Of Everything'. A song in which she said everything reminds her of her man including the seagulls, the airplanes, the sailboats and even the bees. I would love to see what this bloke looked like.

1971

With the move across the sea to Ireland for the 1971 contest came a change in the voting – this time in an attempt to try to keep up with the changing trends in youth music. The new system required that each country only had two jury members – one under 25, one over 25 – who both came to the event and awarded between one and ten points each to their favourite songs. Adding it all up meant that there were 360 points up for grabs. The whole thing was becoming more complicated than an IKEA instruction manual but the EBU persisted and they weren't too far away from getting to the voting system they still use today.

Some of the other rules were changed as well. From now on only six performers were allowed to be on stage, another rule that stands to this day – which means that Kylie Minogue could enter if she wanted to but she could only have five buffed, oiled-up male dancers dressed in leather behind her, and no more.

With all these changes out of the way, it was time to get on with the show. Belgium came out with a typically Euro song by Lily Castel and Jacques Raymond called

'Goeiemorgen, Morgen' ('Good Morning, Morning') in which they spent the majority of their 3 minutes saying just that along with how sensational the world was – which didn't make them sound like Eurovision singers as much as it did Mormons.

Ireland's entry 'One Day Love' had Angela Farrell bemoaning the fact that she had love for a day and then he went away. I hate to be the bearer of bad tidings, Angela, but it's called a one night stand, and you fell for it.

Some interesting lyrics popped up in the Norwegian song by Hanne Krogh called 'Lykken Er' ('Happiness Is'). Hanne says that happiness is an hour in the bath and barefoot in the grass but she kind of loses me when she goes on to say it's also 'letting the cat in' and 'herring in dill'. Oh well, each to their own.

The big winner of the night was Monaco's Séverine singing 'Un Banc, Un Arbre, Une Rue' ('A Bench, A Tree, A Street'), which sounds like it could be the set for a Samuel Beckett play.

1972

Claiming they were unable to provide a suitable venue for the 1972 contest, Monaco handed it over to the

United Kingdom who chose to stage the event in Edinburgh, Scotland.

This year there was more than the usual crop of songs about being in love or being dumped, and that's saying something, since most years that's what nearly all the songs are about. There was the Finnish song by Püivi Paunu and Kim Floor called 'Muistathan' ('Do You Remember?') in which the duo reminisce about the 'first time' – all holding hands and walking together. One of these days there'll be a Eurovision song that talks about the first time and tells it like it is – fumbling around in the dark in the back of your mate's car, drunk on the cheapest, most toxic wine you could con the liquor store owner into selling you because you're underage. Personally, I can't wait.

The Netherlands entered a song called 'Als Het Om De Liefde Gaat' ('When It's All About Love') by Sandra and Andres that took an approach radically different from anything seen before at Eurovision: instead of going the 'la la' route, they went the 'na na' way, giving us 28 of them in the chorus alone.

The Austrian entry, a group called Milestones, offered a cautionary tale with 'Falter Im Wind' ('Butterfly In The Wind'), which warned over and over in the chorus not to stay in the woods. This made it sound more like ad copy you'd see on the movie posters for an eighties slasher flick than a love song.

Malta kept the love theme going with a song called, appropriately enough, 'L'imhabba' ('Love') by duo Helen and Joseph who asked wise men, philosophers and poets the big question 'What is love?' Their answer? 'Love is a kiss, as sweet as sugar'. Lovely. But I don't really buy the next bit where they ask the same question of freaks, hippies and Hell's Angels and get the same reply. I can't see some humungous, hairy guy in a bandana and leather jacket, called Crusher, swinging a motorcycle chain around his head, saying 'love is a kiss' but maybe I'm just a cynic.

Norway's song for that year was called 'Småting' ('Little Things') performed by Grethe Kausland and Benny Borg. Although the writing is actually credited to somebody else, with lines like 'inherit a castle we can' and 'land on the moon we can', I can't help thinking that it was actually penned by Yoda.

Luxembourg took the honours with Vicky Léandros singing 'Après Toi' ('After You') so the carnival packed up and headed to Luxembourg City for the 1973 contest.

1973

Naturally, it wouldn't be a Eurovision without at least one change in the rules. This year it was the language rule. No, that doesn't mean that contestants were now allowed to swear in the songs (although that would be something, wouldn't it?). It meant each country could choose which language they sang their song in, and were no longer restricted to their national languages.

For the first time, too, a non-European country took part – Israel. Which brings me to one of the most oft-asked questions to do with Eurovision, 'If it's *Euro*-vision, how can countries like Israel and Turkey take part?' Simple. The criteria for entering the contest stipulate that in order to enter you have to be a paying member of the Eurovision Broadcasting Union (EBU), which Turkey and Israel are. It doesn't have anything to do with just being a country in Europe. So, there you go, something to amaze your friends at the pub with.

This year Cliff Richard made a return to the contest with his song for the United Kingdom called 'Power To All Our Friends'. According to the lyrics, those friends include the bees, the vine, the land and the sun. Methinks Cliff might have been guzzling a bit too much of that sacramental wine come communion time. While I'm on a theological note, in the song Cliff talks about all the girls he knew before – I'm assuming he doesn't mean that in the biblical sense. And while Cliff, who is often accused of doing middle-of-the-road music, does manage to rock it up a bit in the middle eight of this song, it has to be said that after seeing the performance, Cliff is to rock'n'roll what the Partridge Family are to heavy metal.

Lyrics have always been a source of great fun at Eurovision and this year was no exception. Norway get a nod for their song 'It's Just A Game' by The Bendik Singers. In it they say, 'we're giving it our all and just living and balling'. Now, one assumes they mean 'having a ball' but in the United States 'balling' has a whole different connotation – which I'm sure you can work out for yourselves. Sweden should also have been rewarded for one of the most bizarre lines in a song for their effort 'You're Summer' by The Nova and The Dolls – 'your breasts are like swallows in nestling'. Does that mean they chirp and have feathers on them?

The group Mocedades performed for Spain with their song 'Eres Tú' ('You Are'), a phrase which is repeated over and over throughout the song. For a while there I didn't think I was watching a

Eurovision performance so much as a fight in a primary school playground. It was yet another song telling someone how special they are, with lines like 'you are the fire in my fireplace' and 'you are the wheat in my bread'. With the 3 minute time restriction, the group didn't manage to get to the lines, 'you are the coin rattling around in my vacuum cleaner', and, 'you are the lumpy bits in my milk when it's past its use-by date'.

Belgium deserve some plaudits for bringing topical relationships into their song 'Baby Baby' by Nicole and Hugo. They say 'it's lovely to be together and the divorce doesn't hurt after all'. Good to see a mature attitude but then they go and blow it with another line that says 'I know a woman can't do anything alone'. Try and perform that one today, guys. I dare you.

For the second year running, Luxembourg won. This time with a song entitled 'Tu Te Reconnaîtras' ('You'll Recognise Yourself') by Anne-Marie David who tells us that we will recognise ourselves in everything we see, be it the student who the teacher punishes or the dreams of an artist. If she included a line that said 'in the guy fumbling in his pocket for change so he can buy a kebab after closing time', then I'd recognise myself in that bloke.

1974

After their second win in a row, Luxembourg declined to host the following year. Again the BBC jumped to the fore and the 1974 Eurovision Song Contest was held in Brighton, England. It came as no surprise to anyone that the voting was changed again, basically going back to the old ten-member jury, one vote per member routine for each country. Ooh, but they were getting very close to getting it right.

France pulled out a few days before the contest due to the death of their President, Georges Pompidou. But the show must go on . . . and it did. Quite apart from featuring Australia's own Olivia Newton-John, coming in equal fourth place for the United Kingdom with 'Long Live Love', this was the year that spawned the most successful band ever to come out of Eurovision – ABBA.

With their silver boots and matching stylish knickerbocker ensembles and, of course, their song 'Waterloo', they won the contest and went on to international stardom. Interestingly, this wasn't their first attempt at Eurovision. They had entered Sweden's national finals the year before with their song 'Ring

Ring' but didn't make the cut. They got their own back when 'Ring Ring' went on to be an international hit as well: even the people voting for the national finals get it wrong regularly . . . I mean, occasionally.

Eurovision 1974 is mostly known for ABBA's involvement but it's also important for having one of my favourite band names – Poogy. They competed for Israel with 'Natati La Khaiai' ('I Gave Her My Life') which asks that well-worn philosophical question, 'Which came first, the egg or the apple?' This is a question that has plagued me for some time.

It's not often that you can get some constructive advice from a song at Eurovision but that's exactly what you got from Peret with his song for Spain called 'Canta Y Sé Feliz' ('Sing And Be Happy'). Apart from telling you to sing a lot to feel good, he also points out that 'if you stop for a blonde girl when you're on the motorway but it appears to be a hitch-hiker, it's useless, it's useless, it's useless, it's useless'. Now, I have absolutely no bloody idea what he's talking about but I know that the next time I'm barrelling down the highway and I see a blonde girl, I'm not going to stop because I know now that (all together now) 'it's useless, it's useless, it's useless, it's useless'. Who says Eurovision isn't educational?

The 1974 Eurovision Song Contest was also central

to a military coup that was being planned in Portugal. The cue to start the uprising was a broadcast of its Eurovision entry on national radio. The song was 'E Depois Do Adeus' ('And After The Farewell') by Paulo de Carvalho. Just as well it wasn't the 1998 Portugese entry 'Se Eu Te Pudesse Abraçar'. Somehow I don't think a battalion of burly, armed soldiers command the same kind of awe if they're attacking to the tune of 'If Only I Could Embrace You'.

(The coup did take place and it unseated the right-wing dictatorship that had been in control for 40 years. See what the power of a song can do.)

1975

Stockholm hosted the 1975 contest and yes, finally the Eurovision people got the voting system worked out. Having decided that previous years' attempts at sorting out the voting had been about as useful as a hair dryer in a wind tunnel, they came up with the system of each country giving 12 points to its favourite song, ten to the next, eight to the one after that and so on down to one point. This system is still working today. That is the last time I will ever mention the rules of voting. (I hear a collective sigh across the land.)

This year saw the highest number of countries yet take part in the contest – 19. It was also the last time that any artist would appear on the Eurovision stage three years in a row. It had happened before with Lys Assia for Switzerland and Corry Brokken for the Netherlands in the fifties, and Udo Jürgens for Austria in the sixties. Now Ellen Nikolaysen would do it for the last time for Norway (she had been a part of The Bendik Singers for the two previous years). Nobody else has repeated or surpassed this feat, so if you're looking for a record to break . . .

Cliff Richard didn't make it for the United Kingdom but his back-up band, The Shadows, went instead. Their song 'Let Me Be The One' was marred by Bruce Welch fluffing the second line of the song on live television. Obviously, he took the song to mean 'Let Me Be The One To Stuff It Up', yet they did manage to come second.

Germany's entry by Joy Fleming went for the analogy that 'Ein Lied Kann Eine Brücke Sein' ('A Song Can Be A Bridge'). OK, I'll buy it with lines like 'each tone is like a stone, making it strong and stable' but when we get to 'you can walk over it', that's were I start to worry. Call me a wimp but if I were driving a car, I'd much rather risk it on the Sydney Harbour Bridge than 'A Bridge Over Troubled Water'. On the other side of the coin, Sophie from Monaco sang

'Une Chanson C'est Une Lettre' ('A Song Is A Letter') that 'you write in your head. That stays in your head. That crumples and dies'. Cheery little minx, isn't she?

The resounding winner for that year was the Netherlands with their song ('Ding-Dinge-Dong') by the group Teach-In. With lyrics like 'tick-a-tick-a-tack', 'bim-bam-bom' and not forgetting 'ding-a-dong', it's hard not to imagine that it was written by Spike Milligan for *The Goon Show*. It was the fourth win for the Netherlands and their last so far.

1976

Spain's entry in the 1976 song contest was called 'Sobran las palabras' ('Words Are Unnecessary') sung by Braulio. Translating it from the Spanish, he is saying to his lover that he prefers the 'eloquence of a silence to a used phrase which means nothing in my heart'. Translating that into bloke-speak he's saying, 'shut up, I'm watching the telly'.

A protest song also managed to slip its way in between the 'na na na's' and the 'la la la's'. Greece's entry by Mariza Koch was called 'Panaghia Mou, Panaghia Mou' ('My Lady, My Lady') and talked about refugees and shattered ruins caused by napalm and fresh dug land plunged with crosses that time putrifies. Protest songs aren't really big at Eurovision and this song was no different. Out of the 18 countries performing in the Netherlands, it came in fifteenth.

Diametrically opposed to that song was the winning entry from the United Kingdom by Brotherhood Of Man called 'Save Your Kisses For Me'. The song sounds like it could be a mouthwash commercial but nonetheless went on to sell over six million copies worldwide. I understand the intention of the song but there is still something decidedly suspect about the last line, 'save your kisses for me even though you're only three'. I still shudder when I hear it.

To give them their credit though, they did do something that doesn't happen very often at Eurovision. They managed to win despite being the first act to perform on the night. The Netherlands also managed it in 1975 but it hasn't happened a lot since.

1977

With the 1977 contest moving back to the United Kingdom, there was another rule change. (I said I wouldn't mention the rules of voting again, not the general rules. They would still change more often than Paris Hilton's partners.) This time, it was back to the language rule. Again, a performer could only sing in one of the languages of their own country. However, Belgium and Germany were allowed to enter English language songs as they had already chosen their entries before the rule had been re-established. Ya gotta be quick!

During the seventies Europe was frequently affected by industrial strife, and in 1975 due to a cameramen's and technicians' strike at the BBC things were looking shaky for the contest, but five weeks later up it popped proving that nothing can stop the Eurovision Song Contest from boom bang-a-banging on. Which leads me to the Austrian song 'Boom Boom Boomerang', performed by the group Schmetterlinge. The rule was that you had to perform in one of your own country's languages, so it seemed that they must speak gibberish in Austria. The lyrics talk about boomerangs and didgeridoos but just what the hell is a 'snadderydang'? No one else could work it out either – they came second last.

As usual, love songs played a major part with Norway going the whole hog in their song called 'Casanova', performed by Anita Skorgan. She sings that she is married to a Don Juan who tells her that he is going out for a walk but now she's a bit doubtful as his suit and car are gone. I wonder if it hurt when she had 'loser' tattooed on her forehead?

Heddy Lester from the Netherlands sang about 'De Mallemolen' ('The Merry-Go-Round') and informed us that on this 'merry-go-round of life, your horse is never empty for a long time'. Deeply profound stuff. I can relate to this as a metaphor for my own life – most of the time I'm going round in circles and the rest of the time I'm dizzy and wanting to throw up.

For the fifth time (and last, to date) France won with 'L'Oiseau Et L'Enfant' ('The Bird And The Child') sung by Marie Myriam, a simple number exclaiming that 'love is you, me, the bird and the child'. That might be OK for France but I'm pretty sure that sort of thing is illegal in most European countries.

1978

A record number of countries trouped to Paris to take part in the 1978 contest. After 11 years Denmark returned and Turkey came back as well, lifting the number of participants to 20.

In keeping with their by now established habit of bringing odd songs to the party, Austria didn't disappoint with their entry 'Mrs Caroline Robinson', performed by Springtime. Apparently Mrs Robinson likes telepathy and television, sulphur, Chanel and Bach.

All sounding relatively normal until we learn she has 'sex appeal instead of the broomstick ever since she dropped off her broom'. Right, that's it. I'm getting somebody to go to Austria and test the water.

To prove that Austria weren't the only loopy ones, Portugal leapt into the fray with a song from the group Gemini called 'Dai Li Dou' in which they sang just that for a few minutes before moving on to how great it would be to be a kite. I wonder if when that bloke has finished testing in Austria he could pop over to Portugal?

Israel were the big winners on the night, being awarded five consecutive '12 points', which is still a Eurovision record. When it was looking obvious that Israel was going to win, the company broadcasting the contest in Jordan pulled the plug on the live transmission, claiming they had technical difficulties. To make matters worse, a day later they announced that the winning song was the Belgian entry which had, in fact, come second.

1979

For the 1979 extravaganza held in Jerusalem, security was extremely tight – *remembering that this was the seventies* – but fortunately nothing untoward happened. That is, unless you consider disco entering Eurovision untoward. It hit in a big way with Denmark's song 'Disco Tango', performed by Tommy Seebach. With flares flaring and mirror balls twinkling (not Tommy's, the ones on the ceiling), Tommy sang of the disco diva who leads a dog's life but wants to boogie at night.

The state of the economy made its way into the contest with a song from the Netherlands called 'Colorado', sung by Xandra. She yearned to go to the American state because the dollar is good and 'we can buy a secondhand horse and save petrol'. I assume she meant save *on* petrol. No point in buying a good horse if you're only going to load it up with barrels of unnecessary petrol, I always say.

The United Kingdom tried again with one of its little storytelling songs. This time it was 'Mary Ann' by Black Lace and it told of a bloke, who's been dating Mary Ann, who goes out and gets drunk and sleeps with someone else. Later, a friend of Mary Ann's turns up threatening to dob him in and he starts crying his eyes out. Be a man, pal and accept the consequences. You shouldn't stoke the fire if you're afraid of the heat, ya big girl!

In the Portugese song 'Sobe, Sobe, Balão Sobe' ('Rise,

Rise, Balloon Rise') Manuela Bravo tells us that she likes living in a dream as she doesn't 'need a visa or a passport'. In dreams you also don't need money, food, oxygen or any number of things, that's why they're called dreams, Manuela. She probably dreamed of winning the Eurovision. Well, she can dream on – she came ninth.

Laurent Vaguener from Monaco sang 'Notre Vie C'est La Musique' ('Our Life Is Music'), declaring his love for rock'n'roll, blues music, Saturday nights in Paris, walking along the boulevard and motorcycles. This guy went in the wrong door. He wasn't looking for the Eurovision Song Contest, he was looking for a dating agency.

On the night, Spain was the last country to cast its votes. They were one point in the lead but when they gave ten points to Israel it was all over and Israel won for the second year running with their song 'Hallelujah' performed by Gali Atari and Milk and Honey. That must have really pissed them off in Jordan.

The seventies saw two major musical influences explode on to the music scene. Punk and disco. As different as chalk and cheese. Unfortunately, punk would never be the sort of thing that would turn up at

Eurovision (more's the pity) but disco could have been invented for it.

With disco's simplistic, happy dance beats and, more importantly for Eurovision, its exceedingly loud costumes, it was a style of music that the contest would welcome with open arms in the eighties. The coming decade would also, for the first time, see the same performer win the contest twice and introduce another performer who would go on to be an international megastar.

THE EIGHTIES

So 'What's Another Year' if you really want to 'Rock Me'?

1980

Having just hosted the 1979 contest, Israel didn't have the means to host the 1980 event. The United Kingdom were asked to step in, as they so often had in the past, but the BBC declined and the Netherlands got to foot the bill for this one. The date picked was 19 April which happened to be Remembrance Day in Israel so they didn't participate. Was it a strategic move to stop Israel from getting the hat-trick? Half the fun of Eurovision is the politics so being a conspiracy theorist, I like to think it was.

Morocco joined in for the first time, and after coming eighteenth the King of Morocco decreed it to be the last time. And it was. Monaco had already withdrawn from the event after a dismal showing the previous year and were never seen again.

The first show of the new decade brought some songs that were well up to the standard set in previous years. Switzerland's Paola belted out a number called 'Cinèma', a fun little song where she reminisced about going to the flicks and watching the likes of Fred

Astaire, Charlie Chaplin and Buster Keaton. Considering this was 1980 and she looked about 25, I'm guessing that the song was written for her. Do you think?

Not to be outdone, Germany had a song by Katja Ebstein, 'Theater', where she sang about the heroes of the stage. Admittedly, how heroic these heroes were is up for debate as the song said 'a hero has to be strong, fight for the right but often he's sick with stage fright'. Maybe the only theatre she'd been to was kindergarten end-of-year concerts.

Travel was big this year at the contest, the Netherlands offering a tune called 'Amsterdam' by Maggie MacNeal who sang that 'all kinds of things are going on in the city where everything's possible' and 'here all the people feel happy'. If you've ever been to a coffee shop in Amsterdam, you'll know exactly why they're so happy.

Still infected with the the travel bug, Greece gave us 'Autostop' ('Hitch-hiking') by Anna Vissi and The Epikouri, in which she tells us that with hitch-hiking you can go where you want. Sure. As long as you don't mind being driven there by an arse-numbingly dull travelling salesman or a Kombi-driving hippy who can communicate with the spirit of Jimi Hendrix. And I speak from experience here.

But it wouldn't be Eurovision without a love song and, of course, there was the required bucketload this year including one from Portugal by José Cid called 'Um Grande, Grande Amor' ('A Big, Big Love') in which he says 'the words in the chorus are parts of the same song which echoes in the galaxies of my illusion'. I get the impression that he might have been with Maggie MacNeal when she visited Amsterdam.

Occasionally, someone comes along attempting a major suckfest (either to the host country or to the EBU). This time it was a group from Belgium called Telex with their brown-nosing number called 'Eurovision', in which they prattled on about what a great event it was and how great it was to be there. The grovelling didn't work and they only managed to get 14 points.

A deep and meaningful number came from Norway with a song called 'Sámiid Ædnan' ('Land Of the Sami People') by Sverre Kjelsberg and Mattis Hætta about the construction of a hydro-electric power plant. In keeping with their track record of crapping out badly at Eurovision, Norway only managed 15 points. You have to admire their consistency.

With a whopping 143 points for his song 'What's Another Year', Ireland's Johnny Logan was the winner of the 1980 contest. This was the first of two occasions when Johnny won for the Emerald Isle, although for this first win he was really an Aussie and it was only after the event that he was issued with an Irish passport. One way of getting Irish citizenship, I suppose. Rather than queuing at some government office, all you have to do is win Eurovision. Probably be quicker too.

We can't leave 1980 without a special note about someone who has become synonymous in Britain with the Eurovision Song Contest. Up until now, Terry Wogan had been a commentator for the big event only three times (on radio once in 1971, and twice on the telly in 1973 and 1978), but since 1980 Wogan has commentated on every Eurovision. His brand of quick, ascerbic wit has made the event a must-see for millions of Britons each year. Good on ya, Tezza. May you get to insult many more people in many more contests to come.

1981

Nineteen eighty-one saw the musical circus hit Dublin and more musical oddities assaulted our eardrums. From Denmark came a song by Debbie Cameron and Tommy Seebach (a former Eurovision winner) called 'Krøller Eller Ej' ('Curly Hair Or Not') in which the duo tell us that 'we love our children, curly hair or not' and 'brown eyes or not'. I assume with the latter they are talking about the optical ones, not the ones that hoons do out of a car window on a drunken Saturday night.

Jean-Claude Pascal from Luxembourg gave us a charming little ditty called 'C'est Peut-Être Pas L'Amérique' ('It May Not Be America'). The majority of the song is about how Jean-Claude's kind of music is from his homeland and 'it tells our own story, our roots and our past'. 'It may not be America but America isn't everything' is just one line of the chorus. So, basically, it's just an excuse to slag off America. Fair enough, I suppose. Everyone else does it, why should Luxembourg miss out.

Riki Sorsa performed the unusual Finnish entry, 'Reggae OK' in which he, an obvious fan of the music style, tried his best to convert everyone else to it as well. Strange though that he should use aggressive terms like calling people who don't like it 'jerks', considering the rasta religion promotes peace and tolerance. Never mind, I just find the whole idea of Reggae from Finland intriguing. It'd be like Welsh rap or Japanese country and western music.

Carlos Paião from Portugal had some advice for those of you who don't think you are very good singers in his song 'Playback'. It was simply that if you can't sing or even whistle, use playback, because nobody sings out of tune when they're miming. Not a big hit at Eurovision, coming in nineteenth but obviously it later provided inspiration for Milli Vanilli.

The 'message' song of the year was the French entry 'Humanahum' by Jean Gabilou. Set in the year 3000 in a galaxy somewhere, it features an old man sitting by a tree who tells children about Earth and how that planet doesn't 'shine' anymore because the people on it invented war and ruined it. Commendable sentiment, but it's at times like these that I agree with the Hollywood producer of the forties, Louis B. Mayer, who said, 'if you want to send a message, use Western Union'.

There was certainly no message attached to the winning song that year, the entry from the United Kingdom, 'Making Your Mind Up' by Bucks Fizz. The song not only sounds like it could be the theme for a cheesy daytime quiz program, the title even sounds like one. To be fair, Bucks Fizz do hold an important place in Eurovision history: they were the first contestants to do the 'rip the skirts off the girls so nobody'll realise how naff the song really is' routine, something that has been copied with a great degree of success in the Eurovision Song Contest ever since.

1982

With a fourth win under their belt, the United Kingdom hosted the 1982 contest and their entry was not up (or down, as the case sometimes is) to Eurovision's usual standard. Performed by Bardo, it was called 'One Step Further' and contained the line 'you could have turned and hit me and I wouldn't have cared'. Politically incorrect now, sure, but just to let you know, if you'd tried it with me, I bloody would have cared.

The love songs continued (if you can call that previous example of spousal abuse a love song) with the Swiss entry 'Amour On T'aime' ('Love We Love You') by Arlette Zola, who warbled 'we can change our nose and our life but above all we need love'. I don't know what possessed her to pick the nose (pardon the expression) but I suppose 'we can change our underwear but above all we need love' would have just sounded silly.

Spain made its way to the mike with their economically titled 'Él' ('He') in which the singer Lucia tells us that she's free from eight to ten, and she doesn't particularly like the bloke she's with now because 'he's serious and you're funny. Furthermore, we can have fun and a drink and I prefer you anyway'. All I can say about this one is – there should be more women like her. Please, come up to me and slag off your boyfriend and invite me for a drink – I will totally understand.

Another 'message' song reared its musical head with the Finnish entry called 'Nuku Pommiin' ('Bomb Extinction') about the building of a nuclear power plant. Speaking of bombs . . . this one did with 'nul points'. But not all 'message' songs end up so badly. The German song 'Ein Bißchen Frieden' ('A Little Peace') was the clear winner by 61 points, maybe because it had a positive message and wasn't such a gloom-and-doom number. Lesson learnt. If you're going to sing about man's self-destruction at Eurovision, do it with a smile on your face and a zippy little tune.

1983

The contest moved to Munich and this year Ireland didn't go. During the early eighties there had been growing concern from many countries about the standard of music at Eurovision, and as a result many of them refused to participate. Italy had opted out for the past two years because they felt the contest was too old-fashioned. But eventually they would all make their way back because once you've been bitten by the Euro bug, you're hooked!

For their return performance, Italy chose an interesting variation on the love song with 'Per Lucia' ('For Lucia') by Riccardo Fogli. In it he refers to his lady by saying 'you will have two arms, like a forest'. Personally, Riccardo, I would suggest that if you want to get anywhere with her you'll need something a bit more flattering, but then again, whatever rocks your boat. Speaking of boats (a pathetic segue but I'm going with it), Spain's entry by Remedios Amaya was called 'Quién Maneja Mi Barca?' ('Who Sails My Boat?'), a question that is asked 18 times during the song. A whole verse is dedicated to trying to find out who braids his mother's hair because the girl in the song wants the same guy to do hers. It won't come as a shock to hear that this garnered 'nul points'.

'Fantasiaa' ('Fantasy') was the title of the Finnish entry sung by Ami Aspelund in which she questions if the bloke she is watching every day is real or imaginary. She watches the same guy walk his dog every day through the park and at one point says 'he touches the dog and I watch jealously'. Trust me, ladies, there is no need to be jealous of dogs. Men aren't. We're just jealous of what they can do . . . (because they can).

Even by Eurovision standards this was not a great year but you had to feel sorry for the presenter on the night, Marlene Charell, who had to introduce each song in French, English and German and, unfortunately, made many mistakes. When she got to the voting she clocked up another 13 errors . . . but who's counting?

Luxembourg took the honours this year with Corinne Hermès singing 'Si La Vie Est Un Cadeau' ('If Life Was A Present'). If that was the case, and life was a present, I'd just like to say there are a few bits of my life I'd like to take back to the shop and exchange – but that's an entirely different book altogether.

1984

With Luxembourg's win (for the last time, so far) the show made its way to Luxembourg City but, sadly, the standard of songs didn't improve.

The controversy this year came when the British entrants, Belle and the Devotions, finished and were booed by some of the audience. It wasn't because of their song, 'Love Games', it was because of the hostility in Europe towards the British soccer hooliganism that was rampant at the time. This reaction would have made sense if Belle and her group had sung 'You're Gonna Get Your Fuckin' Head Kicked In', but they didn't so it seemed a little unfair to pick on them.

Spain's entry by Bravo was 'Lady, Lady', a song about a woman who lives in a small rented room and only goes out at night, wearing jasmine perfume, ankle boots and blue eye-shadow. I don't know about you but it's my guess that this lady, lady is a lady, lady of the evening, evening.

Trains, of all things, were a recurring theme in this year's contest. Kirka from Finland in his song 'Hengaillaan' ('Let's Hang Around') told us 'you can catch the train of life anytime', Jacques Zegers from Belgium sang 'the train of time sometimes stops' in 'Avanti La Vie' ('Go Forward In Life'), Izolda and Valdo from Yugoslavia sang in their song 'Ciao Amore' ('Goodbye Love') that 'you had to catch the first train, I know' and the Italian contestants Alice and Franco Battiato just performed an outright love song to the locomotive with 'I Treni Di Tozeur' ('The Trains Of Tozeur'). It won't be too long before the British send Thomas the Tank Engine to Eurovision wearing a short skirt that the Fat Controller can rip off in the final chorus. Guaranteed winner!

Swedish band Herreys won the evening with their

song 'Diggi-loo, Diggi-ley' which had them singing 'the whole world was laughing as I walked in my golden shoes', and since the group decided to perform in the said atrocious examples of footwear, they were quite right. The whole world did laugh.

1985

With the switch to a Swedish venue for the 1985 competition things still didn't improve. The best thing about this year's event was that finally, after a shocking string of duds, Norway won for the first time with their duo Bobbysocks singing 'La Det Swinge' ('Let It Swing'). I thought it was about the wearing of boxer shorts, but apparently it's also some kind of music.

Controversy did arise at this contest, but not from any of the songs. This time it was centred around the presenter Lill Lindfors who, at a one point in the show had her skirt ripped off. Some claim that this was rehearsed, others that it wasn't and the highly respectable EBU was most annoyed. The debate still rages to this day. No, seriously, it does. Honest . . . Oh all right, it doesn't, but you can't blame me for trying to inject some salaciousness to the proceedings.

The early eighties had been a pretty dull time for

Eurovision, music-wise, but the Eurovision Song Contest organisers can't really be held responsible for that. Since each country holds national finals and allows their general public to select their Eurovision contestant, blame has to land squarely at their feet. Yes, the the EBU can lay down ground rules but they can't dictate who should perform and what song they should sing. Otherwise it would be like Nazi Germany. (Some friends of mine believe that the Eurovision Song Contest is something that Nazi scientists invented as a cruel form of torture but they have yet to provide the evidence for such a claim.)

1986

Norway hosted the thirtieth anniversary Eurovision Song Contest in 1986. France got into the spirit of things with their song 'Européennes' ('European Girls') performed by Cocktail Chic. They raved on about how much they loved all things European, like Paris, Amsterdam, St Tropez and England, but especially Lady Di and Boy George – one destined to never be a Queen and the other born one.

Norway's home entry was 'Romeo' by Ketil Stokkan who revealed that he would never be a Romeo because 'his biggest mistake was to feel you up'. Fair enough. Not exactly a tragedy of Shakespearean proportions but look on the bright side, Ketil, at least you copped a feel, didn't you?

'Runner In The Night' was the United Kingdom's entry that year, performed by Ryder, who told us 'I took your heart like a runner in the night'. This is where I got confused because when I was young a runner in the night was when you went to the pub, had a few Heinekens, went to a restaurant and ordered a curry, then buggered off without paying for it, ergo a 'runner'. Although that didn't seem like an appropriate subject for a Eurovision song. Mind you, Dutch beer, Indian food – very multicultural. I could be on to something there.

Germany's entry by Ingrid Peters was called 'Über Die Brücke Geh'n' ('Crossing The Bridge') in which she extolled the virtues of crossing the bridge and 'understanding other people', telling us that 'good thoughts melt the ice in the hearts of our world'. Good thoughts? Who wrote this? Peter Pan?

This year Iceland entered the contest for the very first time with I.C.Y. singing 'Gleðibankinn' ('The Bank Of Fun'), an oxymoron if ever there was one. They warned 'don't deposit your empty blues in the bank of fun' and 'perhaps you're withdrawing too much from the bank of fun'. Luckily, the song didn't go on for too long otherwise I'm sure somebody would have wedged some of the groups' body parts into the night deposit chute of the Bank of Fun.

The winner was one of the youngest contestants ever to compete in the Eurovision Song Contest, Sandra Kim from Belgium with 'J'Aime La Vie' ('I Love Life'). At the time Belgium claimed she was 15 but it was later revealed that she was only 13. Up until this point there were no set age restrictions for contestants but a rule was to be introduced very soon because there were even younger singers to come.

1987

A total of 22 countries lined up in Brussels in 1987 to compete for the crown for Europe's best (or least embarrassing) song. It was the year when one of my favourite acts performed, Datner and Kushnir from Israel with their song 'Shir Habatlanim' ('The Bum's Song') which consisted almost entirely of them singing 'hupa hula, hula, hule, hupa hula, hula, hule' to a very childish tune. Dressed in black suits, white shirts, black ties and sunglasses, it's obvious they were going for a Blues Brothers feel to their act. Unfortunately, because the song was the kind of thing you might hear on a kiddies' program, they only succeeded in coming across as a sort of noirish Wiggles. I loved 'em!

Sweden kept the kitsch going with Lotta Engberg's 'Fyra Bugg Och En Coca-Cola' ('Four Chewing Gums And A Coca-Cola') which, forget all your metaphysical ponderings, is apparently the answer to all of life's problems. It's so obvious once someone points it out, isn't it? Bung in a couple of 'la la's' and you're laughing.

Portugal chose a nautical angle for their entry 'Neste Barco À Vela' ('In This Sailing Boat') by a group with the distinctly non-Portugese sounding name of Nevada. They sang of 'sailing in an overfull boat' and, amazingly, this boat had a 'childish look'. Does that mean it stared a lot and had a line of dribble running down its starboard?

Luxembourg went the safe route with a love song called, surprisingly, 'Amour, Amour' ('Love, Love') by Plastic Bertrand. For those who can remember, it was the same Plastic who had a big hit with 'Ça Plane Pour Moi' (not to be confused with the rude version 'Jet Boy/Jet Girl' by Elton Motello – I would have loved it if *he* had written a song for Eurovision).

The winner was Johnny Logan of Ireland, with his song 'Hold Me Now', making him the first person to win Eurovision twice.

1988

Destination Dublin, and Iceland get my vote for one of the best attempts at rhyming ever seen at Eurovision. The song was 'Sókrates' ('Socrates') by the group Beathoven, and the lead singer shares with the audience the names of people he worships, including Harold Lloyd and Sigmund Freud, John Wayne, Mark Twain and Michael Caine. Unfortunately, they stopped him before he got to Brad Pitt, Eartha Kitt and some silly old git, and the version about Helen Hunt he only sings when he's out drinking.

Italy's entry went the tender way with their song 'Ti Scrivo' ('I'll Write To You') by Luca Barbarossa, in which our Roman Romeo tells his lover 'I'll write to you . . . your name, written in the snow'. This is just a hunch, but I'm guessing that he's not writing in ink.

Switzerland took the number one position with 'Ne Partez Pas Sans Moi' ('Don't Leave Without Me') although the singer wasn't Swiss. She was French Canadian, with really bushy eyebrows, and her name was Céline Dion. Yep, the very same. There is no rule that a country's singer has to be a citizen of that country. Monaco, for instance, had Tereza from Yugo-slavia perform for them in 1966 and French superstar Françoise Hardy in 1963, and this also explains how three Australians have managed to compete.

1989

The last Eurovision Song Contest for the decade was held in Switzerland and it wasn't without controversy. It turned out that the French contestant Nathalie Pâque was only 11 years old and one of the Israeli singers was only 12. There had been young performers at Eurovision before, but with two in the same contest tempers started to flare between countries (nobody wants kids showing up the adults) and the rules were changed the following year to state that performers could be no younger than 16 years old. The kids would get their chance later when the first Junior Eurovision was held in 2003.

Other performances worth a mention were the Turkish song by Grup Pan called 'Bana Bana', which wasn't a tribute to the star of *The Hulk*, but actually translates as 'To Me, To Me', a phrase that the singer repeated a grand total of 88 times during the course of the song. And Luxembourg had a song simply titled

'Monsieur' ('Mister') by Park Café in which the girls sang about an elusive Mister they are interested in who likes 'show tunes'. Somebody should have told them to give up – he's batting for the other side.

Iceland's song for this year was 'það Sem Enginn Sér' ('What No One Else Sees') by Daníel Ágúst Haraldsson who sang 'light up my path, lustful old moon'. Now, I've heard the moon called many things in song but never randy. Obviously, the rest of Europe agreed with me and Iceland was frozen out with 'nul points'.

For the first and only time, Yugoslavia took out the grand prize with their song 'Rock Me', performed by a pretty girl called Riva, wearing huge loop earrings and shoulders pads you could build apartment blocks on. Not the best song and everyone was quite surprised that it won but, come on, this is Eurovision. What were you expecting? John Lennon?

The eighties were very much the 'me' times. People had money, and the decadence that was the call of the day was reflected in films like *Wall Street*. Yep, greed *was* good. The excess of money was also reflected in the fashion, with day-glo colours, lurex suits, leg warmers, harem pants and hair with enough spray in it to burn a hole bigger than Africa in the ozone layer.

People have said that the eighties was the decade that fashion forgot, but as far as Eurovision went, it was also the decade that creativity forgot. While the fashion of the time was clearly seen in the costumes at the contest, with some of the most garish colours ever connected to the human body, the songs were often quite bland. Missing was the spark and the insanity of some of the entries of previous years.

Thankfully, in the nineties things were going to change with Ireland breaking all records and an Israeli act that was really going to sex things up, so to speak.

THE NINETIES
··

From sweat stains to heaven reigns

1990

In November 1989, after 18 years the Berlin Wall finally came down. Thousands of people flocked to the event and helped tear down this symbol of a divided Germany. And what better place to reflect this monumental moment in history than at the Eurovision Song Contest!

At the 1990 event, held in Yugoslavia, at least three countries sang about the wall coming down. Norway's contribution was 'Brandenburger Tor' ('Brandenburg Gate') by Ketil Stokkan, who sang about the famous landmark that used to be located in the no-man's land between East and West Berlin. Then Simone from Austria chimed in with 'Keine Mauern Mehr' ('No Walls Anymore'), which is relatively self-explanatory and, of course, Germany gave us 'Frei Zu Leben' ('Free To Live'). Sadly, these attempts to put world events to music were to no avail as they ended up with eight, 58 and 60 points respectively.

The winner with 149 points was Italy's Toto Cutugno with 'Insieme 1992' ('Together 1992'). It too was a song about a unified Europe, but Toto had one vital element that the other singers going the same topical route lacked – a groovy white suit which didn't manage to stay white for very long. Poor old Toto was a bit nervous and as he belted out his song, his sweat made the black colouring in his hair run and he ended up looking like a singing Choc Top.

Even with world-changing events going on, that didn't stop the prerequisite songs of love appearing at the contest. Edin Ådahl from Sweden in his song 'Som En Vind' ('Like A Wind') told us he's 'a man filled with visions, stay and touch me'. A line that would see him get a quick kick in the swedes if he tried it on any women I know.

Not to be outdone, Christos Callow and Wave, performing for Greece with their number 'Horis Skopo' ('Without A Purpose') came up with another dodgy pick-up line. This time it was 'I want to dive into your fever', a line not only cheesy but which also sounds vaguely unsanitary.

1991

With the start of the Gulf War, the outside world continued to affect the song contest. (That's the first

Gulf War, not the sequel with the son in the lead role.) Unsure that maximum security could be maintained in the San Remo venue, the organisers decided to move it to Rome. Although I'm sure there are many people who would have liked to blow up the Eurovision Song Contest, it didn't happen this year.

This year also saw more and more 'message' songs entering the contest. The United Kingdom's entry 'A Message To Your Heart' by Samantha Janus informed us that 'half the world was hungry' and Cyprus gave us 'S.O.S.', not by ABBA but by Elena Patroklou, who went on about acid rain and birds dying because we had polluted the Earth. Not the usual 'La-la-boom-bang-a-bang-ploppity-plop' songs that Eurovision was used to.

That's not to say that all the songs were deep and meaningful. Come on, this *is* Eurovision. The Yugoslavian song by Bebi Dol called 'Brazil' gave the encouragement to 'take your shoes off, your jacket and pants. Come on, the game is starting now'. Decency prevented them from telling us exactly what the game was but I can only assume that it was nude Twister.

One of the hosts for the contest was Toto Cutugno (winner of last year's event, and he of the melting head). Sadly, things didn't go well for Toto this year either. I'm not sure whether it was the change in venue that threw our boy or just the size of the event, but poor Toto had problems with all the languages and the whole voting procedure, to the point where the EBU scrutineer at the time, Mr Frank Naef, had to take over during the voting part of the show. To be fair to Toto (try saying that three times fast!), there were technical problems to contend with.

When the final tally was in, two countries had scored exactly 146 points: Sweden with their song 'Fångad Av En Stormvind' ('Captured By A Stormwind'), performed by Carola, and France with 'C'est Le Dernier Qui A Parlé Qui A Raison' ('It's The Last One Who Spoke Who Is Right'), sung by Amina. When this happens a winner is decided by seeing which of the two countries received the most '12 points'. They both did – four times. Then the judges moved on to tally the number of 'ten points' and this time Sweden came out on top, making Carola the winner. (Not surprising really because, as I've pointed out earlier, Eurovision songs with weather reports in them always tend to do well and with a song about stormwinds, well, you're laughing.)

1992

With no walls tumbling down or wars starting, 1992 saw the contest held quietly in Sweden and a return to the kind of songs that we have come to associate with Eurovision. Most notable was Finland's song by Pave Maijanen called 'Yamma Yamma'. Just in case you're unsure if that was the name of the song, it is repeated 70 times. To the point where if you heard 'yamma yamma' one more time, you would have grabbed Pave and yammed something in his yockstrap. And when he wasn't singing that, he was singing about 'old radios with a hundred little musicians in it, impossible to see'. Ah, things were getting back to normal at Eurovision.

Belgium's song was in the form of a request with Morgane singing 'Nous On Veut Des Violons' (We Want Violins'). This song would fit in perfectly if they ever decided to do a musical version of *Silence of the Lambs*. I can just see the 'Buffalo Bill' serial killer character belting out the line about hiding his 'emotions underneath the skin of a blouse'.

More love songs with the Swedish entry 'I Morgen Är En Annan Dag' ('Tomorrow Is Another Day') by

Christer Björkman, in which he sings about a woman who paints pictures that he never sees. Sorry to sound pedantic, Christer, but if you never see them, how do you know she paints them?

Keeping the romance going was Yugoslavia with their song by Extra Nena called 'Ljubim Te Pesmama' ('I'm Kissing You With Songs'). An admirable and tender sentiment, as long as the song you're kissing with isn't 'Smack Ma Bitch Up'.

For the fourth time in Eurovision Song Contest history, Ireland won, with the song 'Why Me', performed by Linda Martin. The song was written by Johnny Logan, two-time winner of Eurovision, making him the only person (songwriter/performer) to win three times at Eurovision. Of course, Ireland didn't stop their record-breaking achievements here.

1993

Twenty-five countries competed this year – the largest number so far – and the contest was staged in the smallest venue ever, the town of Millstreet in Ireland with a population of about 1,500 people. A wealthy resident offered his riding school as a place to stage the event and local broadcaster Radio Telefis Éireann (RTÉ) accepted gladly as this would keep down the cost. The irony of staging the Eurovision Song Contest in a place that usually housed a lot of horse manure was not lost on the comedians of the time.

The increase in countries joining the event came from the fact that Slovenia, Bosnia-Herzegovina and Croatia had all declared independence from Yugoslavia, instantly adding three more songs to the proceedings. Personally, I don't think you can have too many songs at the Eurovision Song Contest, but others, it seemed, disagreed and the ever-increasing number of entrants would become a major problem over the next few years.

Songs of note this year included the Turkish entry 'Esmer Yarim' ('My Darling Brunette') in which the singer Burak Aydos informed us that he used to be crazy and now he's just hopeless. An anthem for a few people I know, me included.

Portugal's Anabela, in her song 'A Cidade (Até Ser Dia)' ('The City (Until Dawn)'), told us about her preference for a good night – 'between a gin and a kiss, we're going from pub to pub'. Where is this woman now? I want to propose immediately.

A feminist attitude was apparent in the Spanish entry 'Hombres' ('Men') with Eva Santamaria describing men as 'selfish, conceited, vain, disorderly and spoiled'. But she goes on to point out that 'if they are not around, we are lonely'. Of course you are. There's no one left to slag off.

None of these entries were up to winning the event and for the fifth time the honour went to Ireland with 'In Your Eyes' by Niamh Kavanagh. With this win, Ireland equalled Luxembourg in being the only country to have won Eurovision five times. This was to change.

1994

Unlike previous countries who had won Eurovision twice in a row, Ireland chose to stage the event again, this time in Dublin. Because it had been a while since rules had been changed, now seemed as good a time as any to make some amendments.

With so many countries wanting to take part in the event, the EBU decided on a relegation system. That meant that those countries that had finished in the bottom seven places the previous year weren't eligible to compete this year. Italy voluntarily withdrew so it was out with Belgium, Israel, Slovenia, Denmark, Turkey and Luxembourg. In came Estonia,

Hungary, Lithuania, Poland, Romania, Russia and Slovakia. Some countries weren't happy with this rule – mainly the ones who had been losing badly with monotonous regularity. You see? Everyone makes fun of Eurovision but they all want to be a part of it don't they, eh?

As Eurovision continued, a certain maturity had been sneaking into the lyrics. Take, for example, Croatia's entry by Tony Cetinski 'Nek'ti Bude Ljubav Sva' ('You May Have All The Love'). There's a line in it that says 'the pillow smells nice but your infidelity is hurting me'. Can you imagine anyone using the word 'infidelity' at the 1956 contest? Okay, it's not much, but it's a start. The line reminds me of a guy trying to sneak into the conversation that he thinks his girl-friend is cheating on him – kind of like, 'that's a nice jumper you're wearing, darling, and you slept with my best mate, didn't you, ya bitch!'

More adult content was evident in the French entry by Nina Morato, 'Je Suis Un Vrai Garçon' ('I'm A Tomboy'), in which she sang 'I know he loves me but, whore, there are days which are hard'. Pardon? I have read translations that say 'fuck, there are days that are hard' but 'putain' is French for whore and quite often used as an expletive. Besides, I can't see the EBU letting that one slip past the net. Otherwise, the next thing you know you'll have Cliff Richard getting up and singing 'Congratu-fucking-lations' and that just wouldn't do.

This year was also notable for its interval act (the performance the host country puts on while the votes are being tallied). It was here that the world was introduced to Riverdance. I'll leave it up to you to decide whether that was a good thing or not.

Ireland won with their song 'Rock'n'Roll Kids' by Paul Harrington and Charlie McGettigan, breaking yet another record and becoming the first (and so far the only) country ever to win the hat-trick. Not only did they win but, with a massive 226 points, their score was the highest ever recorded to date.

1995

With the competition taking place in Dublin again, Ireland became the only country to host the event three years running. The big question was, could they win again and do it a fourth time? The relegation rule stayed in place with the bottom seven of the previous year being booted out, but some of the previous relegatees were allowed to return. This year's less-than-Magnificent-Seven comprised Switzerland, Slovakia,

Romania, the Netherlands, Estonia, Lithuania and Finland – Finland's '94 entry 'Bye, Bye, Baby' by CatCat seemed to have been quite prophetic. It should be noted here that there are four countries that can never be relegated – France, Germany, Spain and the United Kingdom – because they cough up so much money to the EBU and it doesn't pay to bite the hand that's feeding you buckets of cash.

It was a relatively uneventful year, with only a couple of songs worthy of note. Russia's song 'Kolybelnaya Dlya Vulkana' ('Lullaby For A Volcano') by Philip Kirkorov deserves a mention, if only for the title, and the United Kingdom's entry by Love City Groove called, imaginatively enough, 'Love City Groove' which included the lyrics 'we're really making love now. Ooh baby, you know how I been feelin''. I didn't realise that the scriptwriter for *Debbie Does Dallas* had turned his hand to songwriting.

Unfortunately, Ireland weren't to make it number four this time. Norway took the prize on the night with their song 'Nocturne' by Secret Garden. (Trivia note: the violinist for the Norwegian group was, in fact, Irish.) The song itself was unusual for Eurovision as it was mainly instrumental and only had a total of 24 words, none of which were 'la la la' or 'bim bang bong'. Another first for Eurovision.

1996

By the time 1996 rolled around there were major changes to be made because even more countries wanted to take part. So instead of the relegation system they introduced a qualification system. To keep the number of participants down to 23 (including the previous year's winner, Norway) all other countries that wished to take part had to send an audiotape of their country's song to the EBU. A compilation of all the songs was sent out to the jury of each participating country, who voted on them secretly and sent the results back to the EBU. The winning songs were in the contest. Wouldn't putting the names of the countries on the wall and throwing darts at them been a lot easier?

For the second time an Aussie girl performed for the United Kingdom: this year it was Gina G with 'Just A Little Bit'. It contained the lyrics 'ooh, ahh, just a little bit. Oooh, ahh, a little bit more'. I refer you to my earlier comment about the UK's entry in 1995.

Spain, too, were getting amorous with their song 'Ay, Que Deseo!' ('Oh, What Desire!') by Antonio Carbonelli where he claimed that he 'wanted to find the footprints under your feet' and that he would 'follow your footprints of caramel and honey'. Was he trying to romance a woman or was he stalking Caramello Koala?

Belgium got all metaphysical by proclaiming that 'Liefde Is Een Kaartspel' ('Life Is A Card Game'). Their singer, Lisa del Bo, backed this up by saying that life had 'jokers and pokers [?], queens and kings'. Unfortunately, this view on life didn't convince many people and, with only 22 points, she ended up as an Ace who won Jack.

But the big surprise of the evening was – yep, you got it – Ireland won again, with 'The Voice' by Eimear Quinn, their fourth victory in five years making them the all-round winners with seven wins to date. Only France, Luxembourg and the United Kingdom have come close, with five wins each.

1997

It was time to pack the Eurovision backpack and track back to Dublin. There was another change in the selection criteria which would hopefully keep the number of entries down to 25. As always, the winner of the previous year qualified immediately, then another 17 countries were picked based on their average points over the last five years (the total divided by the number of times they had actually taken part). These countries were called the Active Participants.

The remaining seven places were allotted to countries that had not been admitted the previous year but who had broadcast the contest and complied with all the EBU rules and guidelines. This was to work on a rotation system each year, allowing different countries to enter. This group became known as the Passive Participants.

If any Active Participant didn't want to take part, the EBU would go to the Passive Participant list and ask the country on the top of the list if they'd like to enter, thereby always keeping the number of entries at around 25. Got all that? Then I'll continue.

This year was also the year that tele-voting was introduced, but initially only in Sweden, Austria, Switzerland, Germany and the United Kingdom. It was later introduced in most of the participating countries but at this point there were still many countries that relied on the old jury system.

The songs this year were still capable of surprising, especially the entry from Cyprus 'Mana Mou' ('Motherland') by Hara and Andreas Constantinou. It included the lyrics 'Tam, tabadabadam, tabadabadam' which brought proceedings to a whole new level of gibberish.

In keeping with the sexy new lyrics that were making their way into the contest, Austria gave us 'One Step' by Bettina Soriat, in which she complains to her lover that 'sex with you passes by as fast as the Spaceship [sic] Enterprise'. An intriguing simile, although an orgasm at warp speed could be quite fun, I'd imagine. She also states that 'love ain't a bounced cheque'. We can only be grateful that she didn't keep the banking metaphors going and we were spared any usage of the words 'withdrawal' and 'deposit'.

Special mention should be made of Norway's achievement this year. Even though their song 'San Francisco' by Tor Endresen scored 'nul points', this made them the record holders for being awarded zero points the greatest number of times at Eurovision. They have managed it four times – 1963, 1978, 1981 and 1997. Go Norway! You legends!

Broadcasting the 1997 contest nearly sent the Irish broadcaster bankrupt so I can only imagine they were happy they didn't have to host it the next year as the United Kingdom won, with their song 'Love Shine A Light' by Katrina and the Waves. With a staggering 227 points, it became the highest-scoring song in the history of the Eurovision Song Contest, just beating Ireland's 1994 record by one point.

1998

With the rules staying the same and tele-voting kicking in, everything finally seemed to be in place for the 1998 event. But little did anyone realise that this year would garner more publicity around the world for Eurovision than it had ever received before.

The songs, as usual, would bring us some little Euro gems. In trying to emulate the 1995 win by Norway with a song that only contained 24 words, Finland tried the minimalist approach with their song 'Aava' ('Open Landscape') by Edea. It contained the title word, 'aava', 'beauty' and 'greatness', and that was it. Ultimately, the Finnish finished fifteenth.

Diametrically opposed to them was France with their entry 'Où Aller' ('Where To Go') by Marie Line. This phrase was repeated over 40 times during the song. The voting gave them a good indication on where they could go. They finished second last with a measly three points.

The standout performance for me that year was German performer Guildo Horn (and his backup band, The Orthopedic Stockings) and his song 'Guildo Hat Euch Lieb' ('Guildo Loves You'). In trying to prove his undying love for the audience, Guildo actually scaled the set and dangled out over the crowd while he screamed out his song. The sight of this manic man with scraggy hair and a wild look in his eyes, obviously deeply in love, is something that will stick with me forever . . . and keep me in therapy for just as long.

The winner was the entry that caused a commotion around the world. It was Dana International with her song for Israel called 'Diva'. Not that there was anything controversial about the song; it was the artist everyone was interested in. For the first time in its history, a transsexual won the Eurovision Song Contest (well, the first time that we know of, that is), for Dana had been born Yaron Cohen. I can only assume that when he saw that the song was called 'Diva', he thought it would sound better if a woman sang it. So rather than change the song . . . now that's commitment.

1999

This seemed like as good a time as any to change the rules. The EBU decided to allow all the participants to sing in whichever language they chose. Naturally, a lot of countries chose English and they have continued to do so. While this is not always a guarantee of success it certainly opens up the contest to a larger viewing audience.

The other change was to the orchestra rule. Up until this point, each host country had to provide one orchestra and each participating country brought along their own conductor. Now, the host country decided whether they wanted an orchestra or not. This year, Israel chose not to have one. This was a way of appealing to a younger audience, allowing countries to bring a mixed, heavily-produced backing track that was more in keeping with current music trends. (A combination of the two could be nice but then again, I'm an old fart. What would I know?)

While not a landmark year for the songs, I will mention the Spanish entry 'No Quiero Escuchar' ('I Don't Want To Listen') performed by Lydia. I beg your indulgence for a moment. My partner, who is also a big fan of Eurovision, has an uncanny ability to pick the winner. She has picked five out of six since 1998. The one she didn't get right was 1999 and she has asked me to point out that Spain was robbed and certainly didn't deserve to come dead last with only one point. There, Gab, I've done it. Now, let me get on with the book.

The winner was Charlotte Nilsson of Sweden with 'Take Me To Your Heaven', a song that is very Eurovision with its poppy beat and smiley lyrics, and it's one of those songs that sticks in your head. (Scientists have now actually come up with a term for that sort of tune – it's called an 'ear worm'. It burrows in and it's hard to get it out.)

The nineties was a very 'pop' music decade. With boy bands and the likes of Kylie and Britney making it big, it wasn't exactly a decade of innovative popular music, but the music that was in the charts was definitely one thing – it was very Eurovision. So, it's no surprise that during the nineties ratings started to swell even more for the contest.

Of course, the EBU weren't blind to this and when the new millennium started they would do a lot more to capture this lucrative part of the market.

2000 PLUS

From two brothers to two nights

There have been many news stories that have put a major scare into the public, like the possibility of invasion by killer bees. None, however, has fizzled quite like the one that was doing the rounds at the end of 1999. To call it a news story is probably stretching it a bit, since for all its validity it was about as much a news story as was Orson Welles' radio broadcast of 'The War of the Worlds' in the thirties. While that sent America into a major panic, this had all of the world concerned. It was, of course, the Millennium Bug.

People were not going to fly in planes on midnight of 31 December 1999 for fear of crashing computers helping to crash the plane. Stocks of canned food flew off the shelves as people stockpiled for the inevitable new Stone Age. It wasn't so much Beverly Hills real estate that people were looking at as a viable living alternative as tunnels under the hills. And what happened? Nothing. Nada. Zip. Bugger all. The year 2000 was a big anticlimax – Armageddon-wise.

2000

Everything that happened this year in the enter-tainment industry was inevitably advertised along the lines of 'the first of the new millennium' or 'the new century edition'. All this just added to the anti-climactic outcome. Sadly, Eurovision was no different. For all the talk of the new century of Eurovision, things stayed pretty much the same. I know that I have said that I love Euro but, in the same breath, I realise that a show that has gone on for so long eventually has to make some changes to keep up with the times. This wasn't going to be the year. Chin up, little Eurovision campers, things would change – it would just take a couple more years.

It wasn't all bad news, though. There were still some songs that managed to keep up the Eurovision Song Contest standard of mind-boggling lyrics. Most notable was Israel with their entry 'Sameach' ('All Happy') by a band with the perfect Eurovision name of Ping Pong. One line in particular has become a personal favourite of mine: 'Here comes the Sunday depression. I want, I want a cucumber'. I don't know about you, but I have yet to read any medical journal that claims clinical depression can be cured by any sort of fruit. At the same time, good taste prevents me from saying exactly how a cucumber might cheer a person up.

More food was on show in the Norwegian entry 'My Heart Goes Boom' by the group Charmed. The song says 'You were standing in the shadows, looking quite impossible. I lost my mind and popsicle.' Again, another example of linking diseases of the mind with food substances. Something that the psychiatric world should be looking into.

The winner this year steered clear of the whole 'food equates with mind problems' theory. 'Fly On The Wings Of Love' was a big hit for the Danish duo, The Olsen Brothers, with a clear win of 195 points, 40 points ahead of its nearest contender.

This year did introduce two new concepts that were to prove very popular. Firstly, Microsoft broadcast the contest live on the Internet, so if people were prepared to stop downloading the latest 'celebrity having sex with a stripper' video for three hours, they could watch the entire Eurovision Song Contest on their computer. This was a boon for Australian fans as it meant they didn't have to wait until 8.30 on a Sunday night to see the delayed broadcast, they could actually get up at 5 a.m. and watch it live. Don't laugh, I know people that do. Mind you, these people can also tell you the title of every episode of every series of Star Trek ever made, which should tell you something.

Secondly, a compilation CD of all 24 songs was released for the first time. It was very successful and one has been released every year since but this does show how slow Eurovision can be with their marketing. Considering this was a musical show that had been going since 1956, an album seemed the obvious publicity tool. Any 50-year-old, pony-tailed, coke-sniffing marketing guy from a record company would have been on to this years ago.

2001

This year the contest was held at the Parken Stadium in Copenhagen in front of Eurovision's biggest audience yet with 38,000 spectators in attendance. The biggest thing wasn't the audience though, it was – surprise, surprise – a change in the rules. Again it was time to change the criteria for actually getting into the contest.

Up until this year, involvement in the contest was based on the average number of points a country had garnered in the past five years. This meant that if a country just had one bad year, it could affect them for five years and because the calculations were quite complicated it meant they could never announce during a broadcast who would be taking part the following year. Now, nobody wants to watch a fun, live musical show with a calculator in their hand and if you, like me, are as thick as an elephant omelette mathematics-wise, you had no chance of working it out anyway.

Because so many had complained about this system, something had to be done. This was the year of the new relegation system. The top 15 countries from this year's contest would immediately qualify for the following year, everyone else got the boot. (This, of course, didn't include the top four – Germany, the United Kingdom, Spain and France). The remaining contestants would be made up of countries that had been unable to enter this year but were keen to take part in 2002 and had broadcast the 2001 event. Simple, huh? For Stephen Hawking maybe. Never mind, as with most Eurovision Song Contest rules, it wouldn't last very long.

A relatively uneventful year musically, there was one thing worthy of mention. The hosts, Søren Pilmark and Natasja Crone presented the entire show in rhyming couplets. It's hard to find the exact word to describe what it was like to sit through this but 'excruciating' comes close.

The winner was Estonia with their song 'Everybody' performed by Tanel Padar, Dave Benton and 2XL which meant the 2002 Eurovision Song Contest was off to Tallinn, Estonia and a new year meant . . . new rules.

2002

According to the new rules, only 22 countries would take part in this year's event but the EBU, in their infinite wisdom, upped the number to 24 – which made for a very interesting outcome.

This year also marked the appearance of some of the weirder entries to take the stage at a Eurovision Song Contest. First off, there was Slovenia represented by a group called Sestre and their song 'Samo Ljubezen' ('Only Love'). Nothing remarkable about the song and the trio had gone to a lot of trouble with their outfits. Glittery, red dresses with matching high-heel shoes and white stockings making them look like stewardesses on Liberace Airlines. The thing that made them stand out? They were all blokes.

Some people were put out about this but,

personally, I think it was great. If one country wants to send a drag act as their contestant, let them. More of it, I say. And in keeping with the French angle of Eurovision, Vive la différence!

Not to be outdone, Greece sent a group led by Michalis Rakintzis who sang a song entitled 'S.A.G.A.P.O.' (roughly 'I.L.O.V.E.U.'). The four guys moved in perfect synchronicity and, dressed in their shiny black, metallic suits, looked for all the world like they had graduated from the Robocop Dance Academy. Sadly, all this effort went to waste, as they only managed seventeenth place.

With the change in rules, two extra countries had been invited to take part this year. One of them was Portugal, who declined the offer, leaving the door open for Latvia to join in the festivities. This was to prove advantageous – they won!

Marie N, a very popular performer in her own country, belted out a great rendition of her song 'I Wanna'. Starting off the performance in a white pantsuit and matching white fedora, in true Eurovision style the outfit was torn off during the course of the act until she was down to a slinky red dress. This production number was a big hit with European audiences and made her the ultimate winner on 176 points – the first time for Latvia.

Better Latvia than never – my first live Eurovision

Welcome to the forty-eighth Eurovision Song Contest, held in Riga, Latvia, in 2003. This is where I come in – my first time as a commentator for SBS TV. Why send a commentator from Oz, I hear you ask? (And if you said it out loud – do you realise that you're talking to yourself?)

The reasons were, firstly, up until now Australia had been showing the BBC telecast and while their commentator, the veteran Terry Wogan, was fine for English audiences, a lot of his references were very England-specific and, therefore, not really meaningful for an Aussie audience. (Think about it, he was, of course, always going on about how great the English act was and how they should win. This is Australia – even if we're not competing, we still don't want the Poms to win.)

Secondly, if this were any sporting event and we didn't have our own commentators, there'd be an outcry. Look what happened when a certain Australian commercial network telecast the soccer World Cup and used the English commentators instead of our own. The complaints flooded in.

Thirdly, and most importantly . . . they asked me, someone who can still remember the words to the 1967 Eurovision winner 'Puppet On A String', so there was no way I was going to say no. Soccer fans want to go to the FA Cup in England, gridiron fans want to go to the Super Bowl in the United States. Me? Give me Eurovision over all of them. So, not only am I clinically insane, I also know my Eurovision.

If I harp on a bit about this particular Eurovision Song Contest, I crave your indulgence because it is still so fresh in my mind. (They say you always remember your first.) Before I go any further let me just say one thing. If you've never been to a Eurovision Song Contest, beg, steal, borrow or print a plane ticket and go. It is excellent!

Like any city that is taken over by a major event, be it the Olympics or Eurovision, Riga was buzzing. Under Russian occupation until 1992, these guys had embraced the west wholeheartedly. Even to the point of having stripclubs inside their four-star hotels – um, or so I was told.

The city itself is a beautiful place with certain areas, like where I stayed in the Old Town, which still has the ancient architecture and the cobblestone streets, with only the odd incongruous American fast food joint on the corner.

All of this historical grandeur was overshadowed by the invasion of press and performers from 26 different countries. At any given time, you couldn't turn around without seeing a camera crew from some country filming something.

With this many visitors hitting town, it also meant something else – lots of parties. To garner favour for their songs, each country would take over a venue in town and put on a big event (in journalist-speak, that means free grog). In the course of my commentating duties and research, I took it upon myself to go to as many of these piss-ups – I mean, cultural functions – as possible. Some countries combined their events as most of them were only in town for five or six days before the contest and with 26 countries it was impossible to have that many parties in that amount of time. At these do's it was common for the artist to get up and, most of the time, mime to the song that they would be performing on the night. (I still have a vivid recollection of watching one of the performers, who had obviously indulged in a few too many sherbets, get up to mime his song only to fall off the stage into the audience. My suggestion to include this in his act on the night of the actual Eurovision contest was not taken too kindly by his entourage.)

But it wasn't just at the parties that you could hear all

the entries. Every time you turned on the TV or radio or, for that matter went into any bar, pub or shop, you would be blasted with songs from the upcoming contest. The songs became the soundtrack to our stay in Latvia. If I had to pick a song that summed up our stay, it would have to be the German entry 'Let's Get Happy' by Lou. There were some nights when we were as happy as newts. (Note to would-be Latvian visitors: Balsam, the national drink, is a thick black substance that is best left for tarring roads. You have been warned.)

The event was held in the Skonto Olympic Complex in Riga. (Up until our arrival, it had only been known as the Skonto Olympic Hall. It got a promotion for the big night.) As you can imagine, security for such a high-profile event was incredibly tight. Coming from Oz, having to navigate through two metal detectors and a swarm of armed guards was not something I was used to. Even so, we managed to breach security on the very first day, by accident, resulting in a couple of beefy Latvian soldiers, brandishing machine guns, chasing us. Well, they certainly knew the Aussies had arrived.

The Eurovision Song Contest is a huge under-taking for any country, so a director and about 150 technicians were brought in from Swedish television to help out the folks from Latvian television. With a live broadcast of this scale, an abundance of rehearsals

are required and this is where the obligatory controversy started. The biggest band performing this year
were the 'lesbians-make-good-publicity' duo from
Russia, t.A.T.u. (which, for those interested, roughly
stands for 'this one loves that one'). Their arrival in
town threw the media into a frenzy. It was one of the
top stories on the nightly news. Sniffing lots of
publicity, t.A.T.u. pounced. After their first rehearsal,
one of the girls was asked what she thought of the
venue and she replied that the stage was awful and so
was the lighting. Bingo! Instant headlines.

For some reason, this didn't endear them to the
Latvian public. It didn't help either that they were
a Russian band. That whole occupation thing was
still in a few people's minds. Funny that. Later in
rehearsals, Yulia, the girl who had made the earlier
comments was noticeably absent, allegedly due to a
sore throat. (You had to feel sorry for her partner Lena.
She still went through the performance at each
rehearsal and was booed by the audience.) For all their
mock indifference they still managed to jump around
like little schoolgirls whenever they received 12 points
in the final voting on the big night and they were only
three points away from being the final winners.

Because the event is such a large one (have I
mentioned that before?) and there are so many people

wanting to see it, four full-on dress rehearsals with all artists performing to a live audience are held to appease the fans. This also enables the broadcasters to get the footage they need for the recap of the songs they play on the final night.

It's at this point I would like to say something about the much-maligned performers of a Eurovision Song Contest. They are often accused of just having pop singer voices. Take it from me, they can really sing (well, the 2003 entrants anyway). I not only heard them at all the rehearsals but I have some of them on video singing their songs, a cappella. If you don't believe me, you can have a copy, at a very reasonable price. (Although none of them are impervious to nerves.)

On the day of the broadcast there was an afternoon dress rehearsal, which most of the commentators attended to acquaint themselves with the 'postcards', the 30-second vignettes played before each act which usually show the performer poncing around the host nation's countryside grinning inanely. At these rehearsals they even do mock voting with the countries to get the hosts used to it. (By this stage most of the commentators had bogged off to the courtyard where there was a beer truck dispensing complimentary Latvian lager at a rate of knots . . . um, yet again, so I was told.)

When it was time for the big event the crowds poured in to take their seats. And to show just what an organised event it was, alcoholic drinks were available. I don't mean within the complex but inside the auditorium. You could belly up to the bar, buy a round, get back to your seat and not miss a second of the performance. That's what I call civilised.

The house lights dimmed and the familiar strains of the Eurovision theme filled the hall ('Te Deum' by 17th century composer, Marc-Antoine Charpentier – just in case you get asked about it in Trivial Pursuit.) After an introduction featuring strange plasticine animation that the Europeans are so fond of but really doesn't mean anything, our hosts took to the stage. They were Marie N., the previous year's winner for Latvia, and Renars Kaupers, lead singer of Brainstorm who had come third in the 2000 contest. They proceeded, as per Eurovision procedure, to perform a dodgy piece of comedy scripting. (This *is* something the organisers need to look at. Mussolini had better gag writers.) They crossed live to the very first Euro winner, Lys Assia, and to Elton John and even to the International Space Station for a message of good luck from the astronauts. (I know some people will go to any lengths to avoid the Eurovision Song Contest but that's taking it a bit far.)

Finally the show started in earnest. First off was Iceland with Birgitta performing 'Open Your Heart'. A good start for the show as this was no different to any song that you might hear on the Top 40 and showed that not every song at Eurovision consisted of 'La la la' or 'I just boomed my bang-bang-a-bang'.

The next act, however, would show just how different things were going to be at this year's event, as Alf Poier from Austria took to the stage with his song 'Weil Der Mensch Zählt' ('Man Is The Measure Of All Things'). Alf was a sight to behold. A thin, bald guy wearing a black beret and red t-shirt, and gyrating suggestively every so often, he looked like a cross between Frank Spencer from *Some Mothers Do 'Ave 'Em* and Peter Garrett from Midnight Oil. His backup band was also interesting. He had two female vocalists and four life-sized cardboard cut-outs of animals holding musical instruments, including a cockatoo, a bull, a cat and something that resembled a penguin wearing an American flag. It was only the second act of the evening and things were looking good.

The contest moved ahead nicely (I hadn't dropped any four letter words that some of the station heads back home were waiting for) and the next song to get a huge response was Turkey's entry 'Everyway That I Can' by Sertab Erener, a catchy pop song that incorporated a nice, indigenous belly-dancing beat (and even nicer belly dancers). By now, the crowd were well and truly into it, jumping up in their seats, dancing in the aisles and cheering wildly. At one point, I even saw someone in the crowd with a large, inflatable kangaroo. (The guy later came up and introduced himself as an Aussie fan of Eurovision. He had always promised himself a trip to the event and this was it. As for the kangaroo? That was just to show all his mates back home where he was sitting.)

The next big reaction was saved for t.A.T.u. from Russia. As mentioned earlier, the girls had not endeared themselves to the locals with their condemnation of the facilities (even though they apologised later because they realised it was a dumb thing to do). They screeched through their number, 'Ne Ver', Ne Bojsia' ('Don't Believe, Don't Be Afraid'), and got a huge response, with only a small amount of booing. They were one of the few bands that came into a Eurovision Song Contest with an established international fan base and you don't buy tickets to a gig to 'boo', so it's safe to say they had fans in the crowd. Either that or, after the disastrous rehearsals, they got on the phone to relatives and bussed them in for the night.

After them came Spain with Beth singing 'Dime' ('Tell Me'), a song I loved, quickly followed by Israel, the Netherlands and then, the duo that was to prove the most controversial act of the evening – Jemini from the United Kingdom with their song 'Cry Baby'. From the moment poor Gemma Abbey opened her mouth she was in trouble. Putting it nicely, she was flat. Flatter than a pygmy under a fallen hippo. By the time her partner, Chris Cromby, came in it was all too late. As painful as it was, I had to feel sorry for her because she had been fine in all the dress rehearsals. Nerves, one supposes, but people vote on what they hear and what they heard wasn't great. Even her incredibly short skirt didn't take my mind off her voice – yeah, alright, maybe for a minute. The eventual outcome for Jemini was 'nul points'. A first for the United Kingdom. British commentators and press all complained that this was a backlash against the 'coalition of the willing' and the events in Iraq. Nice try, fellas. If that was the case, why did Spain, whose prime minister had been all over the newspapers and television with his arm around Tony Blair saying he would also send in troops, still manage to make it into the top ten? Only one British commentator, from their post-Eurovison Song Contest show *A Little Bit More*, stated outright that Gemma sang really badly.

Next up was the Ukraine, appearing at Eurovision for the very first time, with their song 'Hasta La Vista' performed by Olexandr. A truly awful attempt at a pop song but worthy of a mention due to the female contortionist in a blue leotard that performed behind him. Her performance bore no relevance to the song but it did get your mind off the shocking safari suit Olexandr was wearing. Please, don't tell me they're going to make a comeback. I'd rather wear my old seventies purple body shirt than be seen dead in one of those bloody things. The show continued with a noticeable performance from the Polish duo Ich Troje and their anthemic song 'Keine Grenzen' ('No Borders'). Loved the pink hair and the platform shoes and what she was wearing wasn't so bad either. It goes without saying that the Latvian entry 'Hello From Mars' by F.L.Y. nearly took the roof off the auditorium. The Belgian entry by folk band Urban Trad was a very different sound for Eurovision. It was called 'Sanomi', which doesn't actually translate into anything as all the lyrics of the song were in a totally made up language. But I'm sure anyone who has tried performing karaoke at 2 a.m. would have been able to translate it.

They were followed by a groovy little group from Estonia called Ruffus and their very eighties-sounding song about the eighties called, inventively enough, 'Eighties Coming Back', and by the time we got to the last performance of the evening, Karmen from Slovenia, her song 'Na-na-na' although sounding very Eurovision was, compared to the rest of the evening, already beginning to sound very dated.

As telephone lines opened up all over Europe, except in Russia – they still have a jury as they don't have the proper telephone infrastructure – the interval act got underway. This year they didn't have live onstage performers, Latvia instead opting for a series of video clips showing some of their most popular artists including hosts Marie N. and Renars with his band, Brainstorm doing their Beatles 'Get Back' bit and performing on a rooftop. Mind you, it wasn't a bad little song either . . . 'dum-de-dum, be-fore to-morrow'. See it's been this long and I can still remember it. Sort of.

Once that was finished, the voting got underway. Most of it went without a hitch (apart from the odd 'oops, cocked that up – I'll have to start from the beginning' which you get from one country every year) and three songs vied for top place: Turkey, Belgium and Russia. When the final vote was cast, Turkey were the winners. With that inevitable pause, only covered by audience screaming, the artists made their way to the stage to reprise their winning song and Eurovision 2003 was over.

That only left the after-show party which was fantastic but unfortunately, due to legal restrictions, I can't go into detail. Something about 'libel' and 'slander' or something like that. However, the next time you see me in a pub, shout me a beer and I'll tell you all the juicy details. Just don't tell my lawyers.

The outcome of the 2003 contest did bring up some interesting things about the way Eurovision is heading. Take the songs that came in the top five – one was culturally based, admittedly incorporating a pop beat (Turkey), one was a folk song (Belgium), one was a very modern-sounding pop number (Russia) and one was a slow-moving ballad (Norway). Only Sweden with their song 'Give Me Your Love' performed by Fame (those legs! – hers, not his) bore any resemblance to a typical Eurovision winner (and that was only because Sweden are constantly entering ABBA-sounding songs in the hope of recapturing that former glory). So four of the top five were actually very different sounding songs. (Even Alf Poier from Austria with his weird song that was half Wiggles, half Megadeth came in sixth). In fact, the 26 songs competing were quite an eclectic mix of styles and sounds. This can only bode well for future Eurovisions.

Speaking of which, the 2004 Eurovision Song Contest sees a major change to the whole presentation of the event. From now on (until further notice, you know what the EBU is like with its rule changes), the event will be held over two nights. The top ten from 2003 (plus the Big Four, making 14) go immediately into the final. Three days before that, all the other countries will compete in a semi-final, from which the top ten acts will go through to the major event. The numbers will alternate each year depending on how well the Big Four do but it will always culminate in the final having 24 countries involved. So now you get double the Eurovision pleasure . . . I can't wait!

And as if the Eurovision people aren't busy enough, 2003 saw the introduction of Junior Eurovision. No, I'm not making this up. Complete with corny hosts, backstage chats, voting and performances from mini-me versions of their older Eurovision counterparts, the whole thing was like a munchkin version of the real thing but that isn't stopping them from doing it again in England in 2004.

Now even commercial television is getting in on the act. Take a look at a little show that was telecast at Christmas in 2003 called *World Idol*. Contestants from around the world (all from shows where they had been chosen as their country's 'Idol' by the viewing public, that is, their national finals) gathered together in London to perform. The world was given the chance to vote for who they think should be the 'World Idol'. After the votes had been tallied, the hosts crossed to a guest presenter from each participating country to ask for their results in ascending order. Basically, this is just a Eurovision that the Americans have a chance of winning, but they still didn't. Norway did. Go Europe! At least the real Eurovision has original songs, not just cover versions.

There is no denying that to compete with high-profile shows like World Idol, Eurovision has to change and, to give it its due, it has been working on it since 2000, although a radical change is needed if they're going to keep up. The contest can't be blamed for the songs that end up in the final, but the advent of shows like World Idol might attract a different type of viewer to the national finals and, therefore, a different type of winning song might emerge. (I hope it doesn't change too much, though I still want the occasional nutter. Call me a traditionalist.)

The next thing is the presenters. Golden rule: singers aren't comedians. Admittedly, while the scripts they are given aren't 'please get me a surgeon, I need stitches for my split sides' funny, they still contain things that resemble jokes. There's only one thing worse than a bad joke – someone telling a bad joke really badly. It's either get rid of the singers as comperes and get people who do comedy or get rid of the (and I use the term *very* loosely) jokes. Sure, the cheesiness, some would say, is part of Eurovision's charm but that can't help but be there because of the nature of the show. You don't have to add to it. And the only way to survive is adapt. Having said all that (and I've been wanting to get it off my chest for ages – thank you, doctor) I have no doubt that the Eurovision Song Contest will survive – 600 million viewers a year can't be wrong – and I also have no doubt that I will keep on loving it.

I hope in some small way, I've intrigued you enough to turn on the TV on that one night (well, two nights now) in May and escape into Eurovision. And a tip: invite some friends over, invest in alcohol, run a sweep – you'll be hooked. I know I am.

APPENDIX 1

Eurovision Results 1956–2003

1956

Country	Artist	Song	Score
Belgium	Fud Leclerc	Messieurs Les Noyés De La Seine ('The Drowned Men Of The River Seine')	
Belgium	Mony Marc	Le Plus Beau Jour De Ma Vie ('The Most Beautiful Day Of My Life')	
France	Mathé Altèry	Le Temps Perdu ('The Lost Time')	
France	Dany Dauberson	Il Est Là ('He Is There')	
Germany	Walter Andreas Schwartz	Im Wartesaal Zum Großen Glück ('In The Waiting Room For Great Luck')	
Germany	Freddy Quinn	So Geht Das Jede Nacht ('That's How It Is Every Night')	
Italy	Franca Raimondi	Aprite Le Finestre ('Open The Windows')	
Italy	Tonina Torrielli	Amami Se Vuoi ('Love Me If You Want To')	
Luxembourg	Michèle Arnaud	Ne Crois Pas ('Don't Believe')	
Luxembourg	Michèle Arnaud	Le Amants De Minuit ('Midnight Lovers')	
The Netherlands	Jetty Paerl	De Vogels Van Holland ('The Birds Of Holland')	
Netherlands	Corry Brokken	Voorgoed Voorbij ('Over For Good')	

Country	Artist	Song	Score
Switzerland	Lys Assia	Das Alte Karussell ('The Old Carousel')	
Switzerland	Lys Assia	Refrain	WINNER

Note: No scores were made public in 1956.

1957

Country	Artist	Song	Score
The Netherlands	Corry Brokken	Net Als Toen ('Just Like Then')	31
France	Paul Desjardins	La Belle Amour ('The Nice Love')	17
Denmark	Birthe Wilke Gustav Winckler	Skibet Skal Sejle I Nat ('The Ship Is Leaving Tonight')	10
Luxembourg	Danièle Dupré	Amours Mortes ('Dead Loves')	8
Germany	Margot Hielscher	Telefon, Telefon ('Telephone, Telephone')	8
Italy	Nunzio Gallo	Corde Della Mia Chitarra ('Strings Of My Guitar')	7
United Kingdom	Patricia Bredin	All	6
Belgium	Bobbejaan Schoepen	Straatdeuntje ('Street Tune')	5
Switzerland	Lys Assia	L'enfant Que J'étais ('The Child That I Was')	5
Austria	Bob Martin	Wohin, Kleines Pony? ('Where, Little Pony?')	3

1958

Country	Artist	Song	Score
France	André Claveau	Dors, Mon Amour ('Sleep, My Love')	27
Switzerland	Lys Assia	Giorgio	24
Italy	Domenico Modugno	Nel Blu Dipinto Di Blu (Volare) ('In TheBlue Painted In Blue (To Fly)')	13
Sweden	Alice Babs	Lilla Stjärna ('Little Star')	10
Belgium	Fud Leclerc	Ma Petite Chatte ('My Little Sweetie')	8
Austria	Liane Augustin	Die Ganze Welt Braucht Liebe ('The Whole World Needs Love')	8
Germany	Margot Hielscher	Für Zwei Groschen Musik ('Music For Two Pence')	5
Denmark	Raquel Rastenni	Jeg Rev Et Blad Ud Af Min Dagbog ('I Tore A Leaf Out Of My Diary')	3
The Netherlands	Corry Brokken	Heel De Wereld ('The Whole World')	1
Luxembourg	Solange Berry	Un Grand Amour ('A Great Love')	1

1959

Country	Artist	Song	Score
The Netherlands	Teddy Scholten	Een Beetje ('A Bit')	21
United Kingdom	Pearl Carr & Teddy Johnson	Sing Little Birdie	16
France	Jacques Phillipe	Oui, Oui, Oui, Oui ('Yes, Yes, Yes, Yes')	15
Switzerland	Christa Williams	Irgendwoher ('From Somewhere')	14
Denmark	Birthe Wilke	Uh, Jeg Ville Ønske Jeg Var Dig ('Oh, I Wish I Was You')	12
Italy	Domenico Modugno	Piove (Ciao, Ciao, Bambina) ('It's Raining (Bye, Bye, Baby)')	9
Belgium	Bob Benny	Hou Toch Van Mij ('Do Love Me')	9
Germany	Alice & Ellen Kessler	Heute Abend Wollen Wir Tanzen Gehen ('Tonight We Want To Go Dancing')	5
Sweden	Brita Borg	Augustin	4
Austria	Ferry Graf	Der K Und K Kalypso Aus Wien ('The K And K Calypso From Vienna')	4
Monaco	Jacques Pills	Mon Ami Pierrot ('My Friend Pierrot')	1

1960

Country	Artist	Song	Score
France	Jaqueline Boyer	Tom Pillibi	32
United Kingdom	Bryan Johnson	Looking High, High, High	25
Monaco	François Deguelt	Ce Soir-La ('That Night')	15
Norway	Nora Brockstedt	Voi, Voi ('You, You')	11
Germany	Wyn Hoop	Bonne Nuit, Ma Chérie ('Good Night, My Darling')	11
Belgium	Fud Leclerc	Mon Amour Pour Toi ('My Love For You')	9
Austria	Harry Winter	Du Hast Mich So Fasziniert ('You Facinated Me So Much')	6
Switzerland	Anita Traversi	Cielo E Terra ('Heaven And Earth')	5
Italy	Renato Rascel	Romantica	5
Sweden	Siw Malmkvist	Alla Andra Faar Varan ('All The Others Get Each Other')	4
Denmark	Katy Bødtger	Det Var En Yndig Tid ('It Was A Lovely Time')	4
The Netherlands	Rudi Carrell	Wat Een Geluk ('What Luck')	2
Luxembourg	Camillo Felgen	So Laang We's Du Bo Bast ('As Long As You Are There')	1

1961

Country	Artist	Song	Score
Luxembourg	Jean-Claude Pascal	Nous Les Amoureux ('We The Lovers')	31
United Kingdom	The Allisons	Are You Sure?	24
Switzerland	Franca di Rienzo	Nous Aurons Demain ('We Will Have Tomorrow')	16
France	Jean Paul Mauric	Printemps (Avril Carillonne) ('Spring (April Is Charming)')	13
Denmark	Dario Campeotto	Angelique	12
Italy	Betty Curtis	Al Di Là	12
Norway	Nora Brockstedt	Sommer I Palma ('Summer In Palma')	10
Yugoslavia	Ljiljana Petrović	Neke Davne Zvezde ('Some Distant Stars')	9
Spain	Conchita Bautista	Estando Contigo ('Being With You')	8
Monaco	Colette Deréal	Allons, Allons Les Enfants ('Let's Go, Let's Go Children')	6
Finland	Laila Kinnunen	Valoa Ikkunassa ('The Light In The Window')	6
The Netherlands	Greetje Kauffeld	Wat Een Dag ('What A Day')	6
Germany	Lale Andersen	Einmal Sehen Wir Uns Wieder ('We'll Meet Again')	3
Sweden	Lill-Babs	April, April	2
Austria	Jimmy Makulis	Sehnsucht ('Longing')	1
Belgium	Bob Benny	Septembre, Gouden Roos ('September, Golden Rose')	1

1962

Country	Artist	Song	Score
France	Isabelle Aubret	Un Premier Amour ('A Great Love')	26
Monaco	François Deguelt	Dis Rien ('Say Nothing')	13
Luxembourg	Camillo Felgen	Petit Bonhomme ('Small Catch')	11
Yugoslavia	Lola Novaković	Ne Pali Svetlo U Sumrak ('Don't Turn The Lights On At Twilight')	10
United Kingdom	Ronnie Carroll	Ring-a-Ding Girl	10
Germany	Conny Froboess	Zwei Kleiner Italiener ('Two Little Italians')	9
Finland	Marion Rung	Tipi-Tii	4
Sweden	Inger Berggren	Sol Och Vår ('Sun And Spring')	4
Italy	Claudio Villa	Addio, Addio	3
Denmark	Ellen Winther	Vuggevise ('Lullaby')	2
Norway	Inger Jacobsen	Kom Sol, Kom Regn ('Come Sun, Come Rain')	2
Switzerland	Jean Philippe	Le Retour ('The Return')	2
Belgium	Fud Leclerc	Ton Nom ('Your Name')	0
Spain	Victor Balaguer	Llamame ('Call Me')	0
Austria	Eleonore Schwarz	Nur In Der Wiener Luft ('Only In The Air In Vienna')	0
The Netherlands	De Spelbrekers	Katinka	0

1963

Country	Artist	Song	Score
Denmark	Grethe & Jørgen Ingmann	Dansevise ('Dance Ballad')	42
Switzerland	Esther Ofarim	T'En Vas Pas ('Don't Go')	40
Italy	Emilio Pericoli	Uno Per Tutte ('One For All')	37
United Kingdom	Ronnie Carroll	Say Wonderful Things	28
France	Alain Barrière	Elle Était Si Jolie ('It Was So Pretty')	25
Monaco	Françoise Hardy	L'amour S'En Va ('Love Goes Away')	25
Austria	Carmela Corren	Vielleicht Geschieht Ein Wunder ('Maybe A Miracle Will Happen')	16
Luxembourg	Nana Mouskouri	A Force De Prier ('A Request Of Force')	13
Germany	Heidi Brühl	Marcel	5
Belgium	Jacques Raymond	Waarom? ('Why?')	4
Yugoslavia	Vice Vukov	Brodovi ('Ships')	3
Spain	José Guardiola	Algo Prodigioso ('Something Marvellous')	2
The Netherlands	Annie Palmen	Een Speeldoos ('A Musical Box')	0
Norway	Anita Thallaug	Solhverv ('Solstice')	0
Finland	Laila Halme	Muistojeni Laulu ('Song Of My Memories')	0
Sweden	Monica Zetterlund	En Gång I Stockholm ('Once Upon A Time In Stockholm')	0

1964

Country	Artist	Song	Score
Italy	Gigliola Cinquetti	Non Ho l'Étà ('I'm Too Young')	49
United Kingdom	Matt Monro	I Love The Little Things	17
Monaco	Romuald	Où Sont-Elles Passées ('Where Have They Gone?')	15
Luxembourg	Hughes Aufray	Des Que Le Printemps Revient ('As Soon As Spring Returns')	14
France	Rachel	Le Chant De Mallory ('The Song Of Mallory')	14
Austria	Udo Jürgens	Warum Nur Warum? ('Why Only Why?')	11
Finland	Lasse Mårtenson	Laiskotellen ('It's Nice To Be Lazy')	9
Norway	Arne Bendiksen	Spiral	6
Denmark	Bjørn Tidmand	Sangen Om Dig ('The Song About You')	4
The Netherlands	Anneke Grönloh	Jij Bent Mijn Leven ('You Are My Life')	2
Belgium	Robert Cogoi	Près De Ma Rivière ('Nearby My River')	2
Spain	Los TNT	Caracola ('Conch')	1
Germany	Nora Nova	Mann Gewöhnt Sich So Schnell An Das Schöne ('How Quickly We Get Used To The Nice Things')	0
Portugal	António Calvário	Oração ('Prayer')	0
Yugoslavia	Sabahudin Kurt	Život Je Sklopio Krug ('Life Has Completed The Circle')	0
Switzerland	Anita Traversi	I Miei Pensieri ('My Thoughts')	0

1965

Country	Artist	Song	Score
Luxembourg	France Gall	Poupée De Cire, Poupée De Son ('Doll Of Wax, Doll Of Sound')	32
United Kingdom	Kathy Kirby	I Belong	26
France	Guy Mardel	N'Avoue Jamais ('Never Acknowledge')	22
Austria	Udo Jürgens	Sag Ihr, Ich Lass Sie Grüßen ('Tell Her, That I Send My Love')	16
Italy	Bobby Solo	Se Piangi, Se Ride ('If You Cry, If You Laugh')	15
Ireland	Butch Moore	I'm Walking The Streets In The Rain	11
Denmark	Birgit Brüel	For Din Skyld ('For Your Sake')	10
Switzerland	Yovanna	Non (À Jamais Sans Toi) ('No (Forever Without You)')	8
Monaco	Marjorie Noël	Va Dire À L'Amour ('Go And Tell Love')	7
Sweden	Ingvar Wixell	Absent Friends	6
The Netherlands	Conny van den Bos	Het Is Genoeg ('It's Enough')	5
Yugoslavia	Vice Vukov	Čežnja ('Longing')	2
Norway	Kirsti Sparboe	Karusell ('Merry-Go-Round')	1
Portugal	Simone de Oliveira	Sol De Inverno ('Winter Sun')	1
Spain	Conchita Bautista	Qué Bueno, Qué Bueno ('How Good, How Good')	0

Country	Artist	Song	Score
Germany	Ulla Wiesner	Paradies, Wo Bist Du? ('Paradise, Where are You?')	0
Belgium	Lize Marke	Als Het Weer Lente Is ('When It's Springtime Again')	0
Finland	Viktor Klimenko	Aurinko Laskee Länteen ('The Sun Sets In The West')	0

1966

Country	Artist	Song	Score
Austria	Udo Jürgens	Merci Chérie ('Thank You Darling')	31
Sweden	Lill Lindfors & Svante Thuresson	Nygammal Vals (Hip Man Svinaherde) ('New-Old Waltz (Hip Pig Breeder)')	16
Norway	Åse Kleveland	Intet Er Nytt Under Solen ('There's Nothing New Under The Sun')	15
Belgium	Tonia	Un Peu De Poivre, Un Peu De Sel ('A Bit Of Pepper, A Bit Of Salt')	14
Ireland	Dickie Rock	Come Back To Stay	14
Switzerland	Madeleine Pascal	Ne Vois-Tu Pas? ('Don't You See')	12
Yugoslavia	Berta Ambrož	Brez Besed ('Without Words')	9
Spain	Raphael	Yo Soy Aquel ('I'm That One')	9
United Kingdom	Kenneth McKellar	A Man Without Love	8
Germany	Margot Eskens	Die Zeiger Der Uhr ('The Hands Of Time')	7
Luxembourg	Michele Torr	Ce Soir Je T'Attendais ('This Evening I Awaited You')	7
Finland	Ann-Christine Nyström	Playboy	7
Portugal	Madalena Iglésias	Ele E Ela ('He And She')	6
Denmark	Ulla Pia	Stop, Mens Legen Er Go ('Stop, While The Going Is Good')	4

Country	Artist	Song	Score
The Netherlands	Milly Scott	Fernando En Philippo ('Fernando And Philippo')	2
France	Dominique Walter	Chez Nous ('Our Premises')	1
Monaco	Tereza	Bien Plus Fort ('Much Stronger')	0
Italy	Domenico Modugno	Dio, Come Ti Amo ('God, How I Love You')	0

1967

Country	Artist	Song	Score
United Kingdom	Sandie Shaw	Puppet On A String	47
Ireland	Sean Dunphy	If I Could Choose	22
France	Noëlle Cordier	Il Doit Faire Beau Là-Bas ('The Weather Must Be Nice Over There')	20
Luxembourg	Vicky Leandros	L'Amour Est Bleu ('Love Is Blue')	17
Monaco	Minouche Barelli	Boum Badaboum	10
Spain	Raphael	Hablemos Del Amor ('Let's Talk About Love')	9
Belgium	Louis Neefs	Ik Heb Zorgen ('I Have Worries')	8
Sweden	Östen Warnerbring	Som En Dröm ('Like A Dream')	7
Germany	Inge Brück	Anouschka	7
Yugoslavia	Lado Leskovar	Vse Rože Sveta ('All The Flowers Of This World')	7
Italy	Claudio Villa	Non Andara Più Lontano ('Don't Go Far Away')	4
Portugal	Eduardo Nascimento	O Vento Mudou ('The Wind Has Changed')	3
Finland	Fredi	Varjoon–Suojaan ('To Shadow–To Protect')	3
The Netherlands	Thérèse Steinmetz	Ring-Dinge-Ding ('Ring-Ding-A-Ding')	2
Austria	Peter Horten	Warum Es Hunderttausend Sterne Gibt ('Why Are There A Hundred Thousand Stars')	2
Norway	Kirsti Sparboe	Dukkemann ('Puppet Man')	2
Switzerland	Geraldine	Quel Cœur Vas-Tu Briser? ('Whose Heart Will You Break?')	0

1968

Country	Artist	Song	Score
Spain	Massiel	La, La, La	29
United Kingdom	Cliff Richard	Congratulations	28
France	Isabelle Aubret	La Source ('The Source')	20
Ireland	Pat McGeegan	Chance Of A Lifetime	18
Sweden	Claes-Göran Hederström	Det Börjar Verka Kärlek Banne Mej ('It's Beginning To Look Like Love, Damn It')	15
Germany	Wencke Myhre	Ein Hoch Der Liebe ('A Toast To Love')	11
Belgium	Claude Lombard	Quand Tu Reviendras ('When Will You Come Back')	8
Monaco	Line & Willy	A Chacun Sa Chanson ('To Everyone His Song')	8
Yugoslavia	Dubrovački Trubaduri	Jedan Dan ('One Day')	8
Italy	Sergio Endrigo	Marianne	7
Portugal	Carlos Mendes	Verão ('Summer')	5
Luxembourg	Chris Baldo & Sophie Garel	Nous Vivrons D'Amour ('We Will Live Of Love')	5
Austria	Karel Gott	Tausend Fenster ('Thousands Of Windows')	2
Switzerland	Gianni Mascolo	Guardando Il Sole ('Looking Into The Sun')	2
Norway	Odd Børre	Stress	2
The Netherlands	Ronnie Tober	Morgen ('Morning')	1
Finland	Kristina Hautala	Kun Kello Käy ('As The Clocks Tick By')	1

1969

Country	Artist	Song	Score
Spain	Salomé	Viva Cantando ('Long Live Singing')	18
United Kingdom	Lulu	Boom Bang-A-Bang	18
The Netherlands	Lenny Kuhr	De Troubadour ('The Troubadour')	18
France	Frida Boccara	Un Jour, Un Enfant ('A Day, A Child')	18
Switzerland	Paola del Medico	Bonjour, Bonjour ('Hello, Hello')	13
Monaco	Jean Jacques	Maman Maman ('Mama, Mama')	11
Ireland	Muriel Day & the Lindsays	The Wages Of Love	10
Belgium	Louis Neefs	Jennifer Jennings	10
Sweden	Tommy Körberg	Judy Min Vän ('Judy, My Friend')	8
Germany	Siw Malmkvist	Primaballerina	8
Luxembourg	Romuald	Cathérine	7
Finland	Jarkko & Laura	Kuin Silloin Ennen ('Like In Those Times')	6
Yugoslavia	Ivan & 3M	Pozdrav Svijetu ('Greetings To The World')	5
Italy	Iva Zanicchi	Due Grosse Lacrime Bianche ('Two Big White Tears')	5
Portugal	Simone de Oliveira	Desfolhada Portuguesa ('Portuguese Harvesting Feast')	4
Norway	Kirsti Sparboe	Oj, Oj, Oj, Så Glad Jeg Skal Bli ('Wow, Wow, Wow, How Happy I'll Be')	1

1970

Country	Artist	Song	Score
Ireland	Dana	All Kinds Of Everything	32
United Kingdom	Mary Hopkin	Knock Knock (Who's There?)	26
Germany	Katja Ebstein	Wunder Gibt Es Immer Weider ('Miracles Keep Happening, Again And Again')	12
Switzerland	Henri Des	Retour ('Return')	8
France	Guy Bonnet	Marie Blanche	8
Spain	Julio Iglesias	Gwendolyne	8
The Netherlands	The Hearts Of Soul	Waterman ('Aquarius')	7
Italy	Gianni Morandi	Occhi Di Ragazza ('Girl Eyes')	5
Belgium	Jean Vallée	Viens L'Oublier ('Try To Forget Him')	5
Monaco	Dominique Dussault	Marlene	5
Yugoslavia	Eva Sršen	Pridi, Dala Ti Bom Cvet ('Come, I'll Give You The Flower')	4
Luxembourg	David Alexander Winter	Je Suis Tombé Du Ciel ('I Fell From The Sky')	0

1971

Country	Artist	Song	Score
Monaco	Séverine	Un Banc, Un Arbre, Une Rue ('A Bench, A Tree, A Street')	128
Spain	Karina	En Un Mundo Nuevo ('In A New World')	116
Germany	Katja Ebstein	Diese Welt ('This World')	100
United Kingdom	Clodagh Rodgers	Jack In The Box	98
Italy	Massimo Ranieri	L'Amore É Un Attimo ('Love And A Moment')	91
Sweden	Family Four	Vita Vidder ('White Expanses')	85
The Netherlands	Saskia & Serge	De Tijd ('The Time')	85
Finland	Markku Aro & Koivisto Sisters	Tie Uteen Päivään ('Way To A New Day')	84
Portugal	Tonicha	Menina ('Girl')	83
France	Serge Lama	Un Jardin Sur La Lettre ('A Garden On The Ground')	82
Ireland	Angela Farrell	One Day Love	79
Switzerland	Peter, Sue & Marc	Les Illusions De Nos Vingt Ans ('Illusions Of Our Twenty Years')	78
Luxembourg	Monique Melsen	Pomme, Pomme, Pomme ('Apple, Apple, Apple')	70

Country	Artist	Song	Score
Yugoslavia	Krunoslav Slabinac	Tvoj Dječak Je Tužan ('Your Boy Is Feeling Bad')	68
Belgium	Lili Castel & Jacques Raymond	Goeiemorgen, Morgen ('Good Morning, Morning')	68
Austria	Marianne Mendt	Musik ('Music')	66
Norway	Hanne Krogh	Lykken Er ('Happiness Is')	65
Malta	Joe Grech	Marija L-Maltija ('Maria, The Maltese Girl')	52

1972

Country	Artist	Song	Score
Luxembourg	Vicky Leandros	Après Toi ('After You')	128
United Kingdom	New Seekers	Beg, Steal Or Borrow	114
Germany	Mary Roos	Nur Die Liebe Läßt Un Leben ('Only Love Lets Us Live')	107
The Netherlands	Sandra & Andres	Als Het Om De Liefde Gaat ('When It's All About Love')	106
Austria	The Milestones	Falter Im Wind ('Butterfly In The Wind')	100
Italy	Nicola di Bari	I Giorni Dell'Arcobaleno ('The Days Of The Rainbow')	92
Portugal	Carlos Mendes	A Festa Da Vida ('The Party Of Life')	90
Switzerland	Véronique Müller	C'Est La Chanson De Mon Mour ('It's The Song Of My Love')	88
Yugoslavia	Tereza	Muzika I Ti ('Music And You')	87
Spain	Jaime Morey	Amanace ('It's Dawning')	83
France	Betty Mars	Comé... Comédie ('Comedy')	81
Finland	Püivi Paunu & Kim Floor	Muistathan ('Do You Remember?')	78
Sweden	Family Four	Härliga Sommardag ('Lovely Summer's Day')	75
Norway	Grethe Kausland & Benny Borg	Småting ('Little Things')	73

Country	Artist	Song	Score
Ireland	Sandie Jones	Ceol An Ghrá ('The Music Of Love')	72
Monaco	Anne-Marie Godart & Peter MacLaine	Comme On S'Aime ('How We Love Each Other')	65
Belgium	Serge & Christine Ghisoland	A La Folie Ou Pas De Tout ('Passionately Or Not At All')	55
Malta	Helen & Joseph	L'imhabba ('Love')	48

1973

Country	Artist	Song	Score
Luxembourg	Anne-Marie David	Tu Te Reconnaîtras ('You'll Recognise Yourself')	129
Spain	Mocedades	Eres Tú ('You Are')	125
United Kingdom	Cliff Richard	Power To All Our Friends	123
Israel	Ilanit	'Ey Sham ('Somewhere')	97
Sweden	The Nova & the Dolls	You're Summer	94
Finland	Marion Rung	Tom Tom Tom	93
Norway	The Bendik Singers	It's Just A Game	89
Germany	Gitte	Junger Tag ('Young Day')	85
Monaco	Marie	Un Train Qui Part ('A Train That Leaves')	85
Portugal	Fernando Tordo	Tourada ('Bullfight')	80
Ireland	Maxi	Do I Dream?	80
Switzerland	Patrick Juvet	Je Vais Me Marier, Marie ('I'm Getting Married, Marie')	79
Italy	Massimo Ranieri	Chi Sarà Con Te ('Who Will Be With You')	74
The Netherlands	Ben Cramer	De Oude Muzikant ('The Old Musician')	69
Yugoslavia	Zdravko Čolić	Gori Vatra ('The Fire Is Burning')	65
France	Martine Clémenceau	Sans Toi ('Without You')	65
Belgium	Nicole & Hugo	Baby Baby	58

1974

Country	Artist	Song	Score
Sweden	ABBA	Waterloo	24
Italy	Gigliola Cinquetti	Sì ('Yes')	18
The Netherlands	Mouth & MacNeal	Ik Zie Een Ster ('I See A Star')	15
United Kingdom	Olivia Newton-John	Long Live Love	14
Luxembourg	Ireen Sheer	Bye Bye, I Love You	14
Monaco	Romuald	Celui Qui Reste Et Celui Qui S'En Va ('The One Who Stays And The One Who Leaves')	14
Israel	Poogy	Natati La Khaiai ('I Gave Her My Life')	11
Ireland	Tina Reynolds	Cross Your Heart	11
Spain	Peret	Canta Y Sé Feliz ('Sing And Be Happy')	10
Belgium	Jacques Hustin	Fleur De Liberté ('Flower Of Liberty')	10
Greece	Marinella	Krasí, Thálassa Ke Tagóri Mou ('Wine, Sea And My Boyfriend')	7
Yugoslavia	Korni Group	Generacija '42 (Moja Generacija) ('Generation '42 (My Generation)')	6
Finland	Carita	Keep Me Warm	4
Norway	Anne Karine Strøm & the Bendik Singers	The First Day Of Love	3

Country	Artist	Song	Score
Germany	Cindy & Bert	Die Sommermelodie ('The Summer Melody')	3
Switzerland	Piera Martell	Mein Ruf Nach Dir ('My Call For You')	3
Portugal	Paulo de Carvalho	E Depois Do Adeus ('After The Farewell')	3

1975

Country	Artist	Song	Score
The Netherlands	Teach-In	Ding-Dinge-Dong ('Ding-A-Dong')	152
United Kingdom	The Shadows	Let Me Be The One	138
Italy	Wess & Dori Ghezzi	Era ('It Was')	115
France	Nicole Rieu	Et Bonjour À Toi, L'Artiste ('And Hello To You, The Artist')	91
Luxembourg	Geraldine	Toi ('You')	84
Switzerland	Simone Drexel	Mikado	77
Finland	Pihasoittajat	Old Man Fiddle	74
Sweden	Lars Berghagen	Jennie Jennie	72
Ireland	The Swarbriggs	That's What Friends Are For	68
Spain	Sergio & Estibaliz	Tú Volverás ('You'll Return')	53
Israel	Shlomo Artzi	At Va-' Ani ('You And Me')	40
Malta	Renato	Singing This Song	32
Yugoslavia	Pepel In Kri	Dan Ljubezni ('The Day Of Love')	22
Monaco	Sophie	Une Chanson C'Est Une Lettre ('A Song Is A Letter')	22
Belgium	Ann Christy	Gelukkig Zijn ('Could It Be Happiness')	17
Portugal	Duarte Mendes	Madrugada ('Daybreak')	16
Germany	Joy Fleming	Ein Lied Kann Eine Brücke Sein ('A Song Can Be A Bridge')	15
Norway	Ellen Nikolaysen	Touch My Life With Summer	11
Turkey	Semiha Yanki	Seninle Bir Dakika ('A Minute With You')	3

1976

Country	Artist	Song	Score
United Kingdom	Brotherhood of Man	Save Your Kisses For Me	164
France	Cathérine Ferry	Un, Deux, Trois	147
Monaco	Mary Christy	Toi, La Musique Et Moi ('You, The Music And I')	93
Switzerland	Peter, Sue, Marc	Djambo, Djambo	91
Austria	Waterloo & Robinson	My Little World	80
Israel	Shokolad Menta Mastik	'Emor Shalom ('Say Hello')	77
Italy	Al Bano & Romina Power	Noi Lo Rivivremo Di Nuovo ('We'll Live It All Again')	69
Belgium	Pierre Rapsat	Judy Et Compagnie ('Judy And Company')	68
The Netherlands	Sandra Reemer	The Party's Over	56
Ireland	Red Hurley	When	54
Finland	Fredi & Friends	Pump Pump	44
Portugal	Carlos do Carmo	Uma Flor De Verde Pinho ('A Green Pine Flower')	24
Luxembourg	Jürgen Marcus	Chansons Pour Ceux Qui S'Aiment ('Songs For Those Who Love')	17
Germany	Les Humphries Singers	Sing Sang Song	12
Greece	Mariza Koch	Panaghia Mou, Panaghia Mou ('My Lady, My Lady')	12
Spain	Braulio	Sobran Las Palabras ('Words Are Unnecessary')	11
Yugoslavia	Ambasadori	Ne Mogu Skriti Svoj Bol ('I Can't Hide My Pain')	10
Norway	Anne-Karine Strøm	Mata Hari	7

1977

Country	Artist	Song	Score
France	Marie Myriam	L'Oiseau Et L'Enfant ('The Bird And The Child')	136
United Kingdom	Lynsey de Paul & Mike Moran	Rock Bottom	121
Ireland	The Swarbriggs Plus Two	It's Nice To Be In Love Again	119
Monaco	Michèle Torr	Une Petite Française ('A Little Frenchwoman')	96
Greece	Pascalis, Marianna, Robert, Bessy	Máthima Solfege ('Solfege Lesson')*	92
Switzerland	Pepe Lienhard Band	Swiss Lady	71
Belgium	Dream Express	A Million In One, Two, Three	69
Germany	Silver Convention	Telegram	55
Spain	Micky	Enséñame A Cantar ('Teach Me To Sing')	52
Finland	Monica Aspelund	Lapponia ('Lapland')	50
Israel	Ilanit	'Ahava Hi Shir Li-Shnayim ('Love Is A Song For Two')	49
The Netherlands	Heddy Lester	De Mallemolen ('The Merry-Go-Round')	35
Italy	Mia Martini	Libera ('Free')	33
Portugal	Os Amigos	Portugal No Coração ('Portugal In My Heart')	18
Norway	Anita Skorgan	Casanova	18

Country	Artist	Song	Score
Luxembourg	Anne-Marie B	Frère Jacques ('Brother John')	17
Austria	Schmetterlinge	Boom Boom Boomerang	11
Sweden	Forbes	Beatles	2

* Solfege – A way of assigning syllables to musical scales. Come on, you've all seen 'The Sound Of Music'.

1978

Country	Artist	Song	Score
Israel	Yizhar Cohen & the Alphabeta	'A-Ba-Ni-Bi ('I Love You')	157
Belgium	Jean Vallée	L'Amour, Ça Fait Chanter La Vie ('Love, It Makes Life Sing')	125
France	Joël Prévost	Il Y Aura Toujours Des Violons ('There Will Always Be Violins')	119
Monaco	Caline & Olivier Toussaint	Les Jardins De Monaco ('The Gardens Of Monaco')	107
Ireland	Colm Wilkinson	Born To Sing	86
Germany	Ireen Sheer	Feuer ('Fire')	84
Luxembourg	Baccara	Parlez-Vous Français? ('Do You Speak French?')	73
Greece	Tania Tsanaclidou	Charlie Chaplin	66
Spain	José Vélez	Bailemos Un Vals ('Let's Dance A Waltz')	65
Switzerland	Carole Vinci	Vivre ('To Live')	65
United Kingdom	Co-co	The Bad Old Days	61
Italy	Ricchi & Poveri	Questo Amore ('This Love')	53
The Netherlands	Harmony	't Is OK ('It's OK')	37

Country	Artist	Song	Score
Sweden	Björn Skifs	Det Blir Alltid Värre Framåt Natten ('It Always Gets Worse Towards The Night')	26
Austria	Springtime	Mrs Caroline Robinson	14
Denmark	Mabel	Boom Boom	13
Portugal	Gemini	Dai-Li-Dou	5
Finland	Seija Simola	Anna Rakkaudelle Tilaisuus ('Give Love A Chance')	2
Turkey	Nilüfer & Nazar	Sevince ('Love')	2
Norway	Jahn Teigen	Mil Etter Mil ('Mile After Mile')	0

1979

Country	Artist	Song	Score
Israel	Gali Atari & Milk and Honey	Hallelujah	125
Spain	Betty Missiego	Su Canción ('Your Song')	116
France	Anne-Marie David	Je Suis L'Enfant Soleil ('I'm The Sun-Child')	106
Germany	Dschinghis Khan	Dschinghis Khan ('Genghis Khan')	86
Ireland	Cathal Dunne	Happy Man	80
Denmark	Tommy Seebach	Disco Tango	76
United Kingdom	Black Lace	Mary Ann	73
Greece	Elpida	Sikrátí Esú Soúperstar ('Socrates, You Superstar')	69
Portugal	Manuela Bravo	Sobe, Sobe, Balão Sobe ('Rise, Rise, Balloon Rise')	64
Switzerland	Peter, Sue & Marc	Trödler Und Co ('Junk Dealers And Companions')	60
Norway	Anita Skorgan	Oliver	57
The Netherlands	Xandra	Colorado	51
Luxembourg	Jeane Manson	J'Ai Déjà Vu Ça Dans Tes Yeux ('I Already Saw That In Your Eyes')	44
Finland	Katri-Helena	Katson Sineen Taivaan ('I'm Looking At The Blue Sky')	38
Italy	Matia Bazar	Raggio Di Luna ('Moon Beam')	27

Country	Artist	Song	Score
Monaco	Laurent Vaguener	Notre Vie C'Est La Musique ('Our Life Is Music')	12
Sweden	Ted Gärdestad	Satellit ('Satellite')	8
Belgium	Micha Marah	Hey Na Na	5
Austria	Christina Simon	Heute In Jerusalem ('Today In Jerusalem')	5

1980

Country	Artist	Song	Score
Ireland	Johnny Logan	What's Another Year	143
Germany	Katja Ebstein	Theater ('Theatre')	128
United Kingdom	Prima Donna	Love Enough For Two	106
Switzerland	Paola	Cinéma ('Cinema')	104
The Netherlands	Maggie MacNeal	Amsterdam	93
Italy	Alan Sorrenti	Non So Che Darei ('I Don't Know What To Give')	87
Portugal	José Cid	Um Grande, Grande Amor ('A Big, Big Love')	71
Austria	Blue Danube	Du Bist Musik ('You Are Music')	64
Luxembourg	Sophie & Magaly	Le Papa Pingouin ('The Father Penguin')	56
Sweden	Tomas Ledin	Just Nu! ('Right Now!')	47
France	Profil	Hé, Hé, M'Sieurs, Dames ('Hey, Hey, Gentlemen, Ladies')	45
Spain	Trigo Limpio	Quedate Esta Noche ('Stay Tonight')	38
Greece	Anna Vissi & The Epikouri	Autostop ('Hitch-hiking')	30
Denmark	Bamses Venner	Tanker Altid På Dig ('Always Thinking Of You')	25
Turkey	Ajda Pekkan	Pet'r Oil ('Petrol')	23

Country	Artist	Song	Score
Norway	Sverre Kjelsberg & Mattis Hætta	Sámiid Ædnan ('Land Of The Sami People')	15
Belgium	Telex	Eurovision	14
Morocco	Samira Bensaid	Bitaqat Khub ('Love Message')	7
Finland	Vesa-Matti Loiri	Huilumies ('Flute Man')	6

1981

Country	Artist	Song	Score
United Kingdom	Bucks Fizz	Making Your Mind Up	136
Germany	Lena Valaitis	Johnny Blue	132
France	Jean Gabilou	Humanahum	125
Switzerland	Peter, Sue & Marc	Io Senza Te ('Me Without You')	121
Ireland	Sheeba	Horoscopes	105
Cyprus	Island	Mónika	69
Israel	Hakol Over Habibi	Ha-layla ('Tonight')	56
Greece	Yiannis Dimitras	Feggari Kalokerino ('Summer Moon')	55
The Netherlands	Linda Williams	Het Is Een Wonder ('It's A Wonder')	51
Sweden	Björn Skifs	Fångad I En Dröm ('Captured In A Dream')	50
Denmark	Debbie Cameron & Tommy Seebach	Krøller Eller Ej ('Curly Hair Or Not')	41
Luxembourg	Jean-Claude Pascal	C'Est Peut-Être Pas L 'Amérique ('It May Not Be America')	41
Belgium	Emly Starr	Samson	40
Spain	Bacchelli	Y Sólo Tú ('And Only You')	38
Yugoslavia	Seid-Memić Vajta	Leila	35
Finland	Riki Sorsa	Reggae OK	27
Austria	Marty Brem	Wenn Du Da Bist ('When You're Here')	20

Country	Artist	Song	Score
Turkey	Modern Folk Üçlüsü & Aysegül Aldinç	Dönme Dolap ('The Carousel')	9
Portugal	Carlos Paião	Playback	9
Norway	Finn Kalvik	Aldri I Livet ('Never In My Life')	0

1982

Country	Artist	Song	Score
Germany	Nicole	Ein Bißchen Frieden ('A Little Peace')	161
Israel	Avi Toledano	Hora	100
Switzerland	Arlette Zola	Amour On T'Aime ('Love We Love You')	97
Belgium	Stella	Si Tu Aimes Ma Musique ('If You Like My Music')	96
Cyprus	Anna Vissi	Móno I Agápí ('Only Love')	85
Luxembourg	Svetlana	Cours Après Le Temps ('Run After Time')	78
United Kingdom	Bardo	One Step Further	76
Sweden	Chips	Dag Efter Dag ('Day After Day')	67
Austria	Mess	Sonntag ('Sunday')	57
Spain	Lucia	Él ('He')	52
Ireland	The Duskeys	Here Today, Gone Tomorrow	49
Norway	Jahn Teigen & Anita Skorgan	Adieu ('Goodbye')	40
Portugal	Doce	Bem Bom ('Very Good')	32
Yugoslavia	Aska	Halo, Halo ('Hello, Hello')	21
Turkey	Neco	Hani? ('Where?')	20
The Netherlands	Bill Van Dijk	Jij En Ik ('You And I')	8
Denmark	Brixx	Video, Video	5
Finland	Kojo	Nuku Pommiin ('Bomb Extinction')	0

1983

Country	Artist	Song	Score
Luxembourg	Corinne Hermès	Si La Vie Est Un Cadeau ('If Life Was A Present')	142
Israel	Ofra Haza	Khay ('Alive')	136
Sweden	Carola Häggkvist	Främling ('Stranger')	126
Yugoslavia	Danijel	Džuli ('Julie')	125
Germany	Hoffmann & Hoffmann	Rücksicht ('Consideration')	94
United Kingdom	Sweet Dreams	I'm Never Giving Up	79
The Netherlands	Bernadette	Sing Me A Song	66
France	Guy Bonnet	Vivre ('Live')	56
Norway	Jahn Teigen	Do Re Mi	53
Austria	Westend	Hurricane	53
Italy	Riccardo Fogli	Per Lucia ('For Lucia')	41
Finland	Ami Aspelund	Fantasiaa ('Fantasy')	41
Portugal	Armando Gama	Esta Balada Que Te Dou ('This Ballad That I Give You')	33
Greece	Christie Stasinopoulou	Mou Les ('You Tell Me')	32
Switzerland	Mariella Farré	Io Così Non Ci Sto ('I Don't Like It This Way')	28
Cyprus	Stavros & Dina	Í Agápí Akóma Zei ('Love Is Still Alive')	26

Country	Artist	Song	Score
Denmark	Gry Johansen	Kloden Drejer ('The World Is Spinning')	16
Belgium	Pas de Deux	Rendez-vous	13
Turkey	Cetin Alp & The Short Waves	Opera	0
Spain	Remedios Amaya	Quién Maneja Mi Barca? ('Who Sails My Boat?')	0

1984

Country	Artist	Song	Score
Sweden	Herreys	Diggi-loo, Diggi-ley	145
Ireland	Linda Martin	Terminal 3	137
Spain	Bravo	Lady, Lady	106
Denmark	Hot Eyes	Det' Lige Det ('That's Just The Thing')	101
Belgium	Jacques Zegers	Avanti La Vie ('Go Forward In Life')	70
Italy	Alice & Franco Battiato	I Treni De Tozeur ('The Trains Of Tozeur')	70
United Kingdom	Belle & The Devotions	Love Games	63
France	Annick Thoumazeau	Autant D'Amoureux Que D'Étoiles ('As Many Lovers As Stars')	61
Finland	Kirka	Hengaillaan ('Let's Hang Around')	46
Luxembourg	Sophie Carle	100% D'amour ('100% Love')	39
Portugal	Maria Guinot	Silêncio E Tanta Gente ('Silence And So Many People')	38
Turkey	Beş Yil Önce & On Yil Sonra	Halay	37
The Netherlands	Maribelle	Ik Hou Van Jou ('I Love You')	34
Germany	Mary Roos	Aufrecht Geh'n ('Stand Tall')	34
Cyprus	Andy Paul	Anna Maria Léna	31
Switzerland	Rainy Day	Welche Farbe Hat Der Sonnenschein ('What Colour Is The Sunshine')	30

APPENDIX 1

Country	Artist	Song	Score
Norway	Dollie de Luxe	Lenge Leve Livet ('Long Live Life')	29
Yugoslavia	Izolda & Vlado	Ciao Amore ('Goodbye Love')	26
Austria	Anita	Einfach Weg ('Just Get Away')	5

1985

Country	Artist	Song	Score
Norway	Bobbysocks	La Det Swinge ('Let It Swing')	123
Germany	Wind	Für Alle ('For Everyone')	105
Sweden	Kikki Danielsson	Bra Vibrationer ('Good Vibrations')	103
United Kingdom	Vikki Watson	Love Is	100
Israel	Yizhar Cohen	Olé Olé	93
Ireland	Maria Christian	Wait Until The Weekend Comes	91
Italy	Al Bano & Romina Power	Magic, Oh Magic	78
Austria	Gary Lux	Kinder Dieser Welt ('Children Of This World')	60
Finland	Sonja Lumme	Eläköön Elämä ('Long Live Life')	58
France	Roger Bens	Femme, Dans Ses Rêves Aussi ('Woman, Even In Her Dreams')	56
Denmark	Kirsten & Søren	Sku' Du Spørg' Fra No'en ('Would You Like To Know?')	41
Switzerland	Mariella Farré & Pino Gasparini	Piano Piano	39
Luxembourg	The Internationals	Children, Kinder, Enfants ('Children, Children, Children')	37
Spain	Paloma San Basilio	La Fiesta Terminó ('The Party's Over')	36
Turkey	Mazhar, Fuat & Özkan	Aşik Oldum (Didai Didai Dai) I'm In Love (Diday Diday Day)	36

Country	Artist	Song	Score
Cyprus	Lia Vissi	To Katálava Argá ('I Realised It Too Late')	15
Greece	Takis Biniaris	Moiázoume ('We Resemble')	15
Portugal	Adelaïde	Penso Em Ti, Eu Sei ('Thinking Of You, I Know')	9
Belgium	Linda Lepomme	Laat Me Nu Gaan ('Let Me Go Now')	7

1986

Country	Artist	Song	Score
Belgium	Sandra Kim	J'Aime La Vie ('I Love Life')	176
Switzerland	Daniela Simons	Pas Pour Moi ('Not For Me')	140
Luxembourg	Sherissa Laurence	L'Amour De Ma Vie ('The Love Of My Life')	117
Ireland	Luv Bug	You Can Count On Me	96
Sweden	Lasse Holm & Monica Törnell	E' De' Det Här Du Kallar Kärlek? ('Is This What You Call Love?')	78
Denmark	Trax	Du Er Fuld Af Løgn ('You Are Full Of Lies')	77
United Kingdom	Ryder	Runner In The Night	72
Germany	Ingrid Peters	Über Die Brücke Geh'n ('Crossing The Bridge')	62
Turkey	Klips ve Onlar	Halley	53
Spain	Cadillac	Valentino	51
Yugoslavia	Doris Dragovic	Željo Moja ('My Desire')	49
Norway	Ketil Stokkan	Romeo	44
The Netherlands	Frizzle Sizzle	Alles Heeft Een Ritme ('Everything Has Rhythm')	40
Portugal	Dora	Não Sejas Mau Para Mim ('Don't Be So Bad To Me')	28
Finland	Kari Kuivalainen	Päivä Kahden Ihmisen ('Day Of Two People')	22
Iceland	I.C.Y.	Gleðibankinn ('The Bank Of Fun')	19

Country	Artist	Song	Score
France	Cocktail Chic	Européennes ('European Girls')	13
Austria	Timna Brauer	Die Zeit Ist Einsam ('Time Is Lonely')	12
Israel	Moti Giladi & Sarai Tzuriel	Yavoh Yom ('A Day Will Come')	7
Cyprus	Elpida	Tóra Zo ('Now I Live')	4

1987

Country	Artist	Song	Score
Ireland	Johnny Logan	Hold Me Now	172
Germany	Wind	Laß Die Sonne In Dein Herz ('Let The Sun Into Your Heart')	141
Italy	Umberto Tozzi & Raf	Gente Di Mare ('People Of The Sea')	103
Yugoslavia	Novi Fosili	Ja Sam Za Ples ('I Want to Dance')	92
The Netherlands	Marcha	Rechtop In De Wind ('Upright In The Wind')	83
Denmark	Anne-Catherine Herdorf & Drengene	En Lille Melodi ('A Little Melody')	83
Cyprus	Alexia	Aspro, Mavro ('White, Black')	80
Israel	Datner & Kushnir	Shir Habatlanim ('The Bum's Song')	73
Norway	Kate Gullbrandsen	Mitt Liv ('My Life')	65
Greece	Bang	Stop	64
Belgium	Liliane Saint-Pierre	Soldiers Of Love	56
Sweden	Lotta Engberg	Fyra Bugg Och En Coca-Cola (Boogaloo) ('Four Chewing Gums And A Coca-Cola')	50
United Kingdom	Rikki	Only The Light	47

Country	Artist	Song	Score
France	Christine Minier	Les Mots D'Amour N'Ont Pas De Dimanche ('No Sunday In Loving Words')	44
Finland	Vicky Rosti	Sata Salamaa ('One Hundred Lightnings')	32
Iceland	Halla Margrét	Hægt Og Hljótt ('Slowly And Quietly')	28
Switzerland	Carol Rich	Moitié, Moitié ('Half And Half')	26
Portugal	Nevada	Neste Barco À Vela ('In This Sailing Boat')	15
Spain	Patricia Kraus	No Estas Solo ('You're Not Alone')	10
Austria	Gary Lux	Nur Noch Gefühl ('Only Feelings')	8
Luxembourg	Plastic Bertrand	Amour, Amour ('Love, Love')	4
Turkey	Seyyal Taner & Locomotif	Şarkim Sevgi Üstüne ('My Song Is About Love')	0

1988

Country	Artist	Song	Score
Switzerland	Céline Dion	Ne Partez Pas Sans Moi ('Don't Leave Without Me')	137
United Kingdom	Scott Fitzgerald	Go	136
Denmark	Hot Eyes	Ka' Du Se Hva' Jeg Sa' ('Can You See What I Said')	92
Luxembourg	Lara Fabian	Croire ('Believing')	90
Norway	Karoline Krüger	For Vår Jord ('For Our Earth')	88
Yugoslavia	Silver Wings	Mangup ('Rascal')	87
Israel	Yardena Arazi	Ben Adam ('Human')	85
Ireland	Jump The Gun	Take Him Home	79
The Netherlands	Gerard Joling	Shangri-La	70
France	Gérard Lenorman	Chanteur De Charme ('Charm Singer')	64
Spain	La Decada	La Chica Que Yo Quiero ('The Girl That I Want')	58
Italy	Luca Barbarossa	Ti Scrivo ('I'll Write To You')	52
Sweden	Tommy Körberg	Stad I Ljus ('City Of Light')	52
Germany	Chris & Maxi Garden	Lied Für Einen Freund ('Song For A Friend')	48
Turkey	Mazhar, Fuat & Özkan	Sufi	37
Iceland	Beathoven	Sókrates ('Socrates')	20

Country	Artist	Song	Score
Greece	Afroditi Fryda	Klóoun ('Clown')	10
Belgium	Reynaert	Laissez Briller Le Soleil ('Let The Sun Shine')	5
Portugal	Dora	Voltarei ('I Will Return')	5
Finland	Boulevard	Nauvravat Silmät Muistetaan ('Laughing Eyes Are Remembered')	3
Austria	Wilfried	Lisa, Mona Lisa	0

1989

Country	Artist	Song	Score
Yugoslavia	Riva	Rock Me	137
United Kingdom	Live Report	Why Do I Always Get It Wrong?	130
Denmark	Birthe Kjær	Vi Maler Byen Rød ('We Paint The City Red')	111
Sweden	Tommy Nilsson	En Dag ('One Day')	110
Austria	Thomas Forstner	Nur Ein Lied ('Just A Song')	97
Spain	Nina	Nacida Para Amar ('Born To Love')	88
Finland	Anneli Saaristo	La Dolce Vita ('The Good Life')	76
France	Nathalie Pâque	J'Ai Volé La Vie ('I Stole Life')	60
Greece	Marianna Efstratiou	Tó Dikó Sou Astéri ('Your Own Star')	56
Italy	Anna Oxa & Fausto Leali	Avrei Voluto ('I Would've Wanted')	56
Cyprus	Yiannis Savidakis & Fanny Polymeri	Apópse As Brethoúme ('Let's Meet Tonight')	51
Israel	Gili & Galit	Derekh Ha'Melekh ('The King's Road')	50
Switzerland	Furbaz	Viver Senza Tei ('To Live Without You')	47
Germany	Nino de Angelo	Flieger ('Flyers')	46
The Netherlands	Justine Pelmelay	Blijf Zoals Je Bent ('Stay The Way You Are')	45

Country	Artist	Song	Score
Portugal	Da Vinci	Conquistador ('Conqueror')	39
Norway	Britt Synnøve Johansen	Venners Nærhet ('The Closeness Of Friends')	30
Ireland	Kiev Connoly	The Real Me	21
Belgium	Ingeborg	Door De Wind ('Through The Wind')	13
Luxembourg	Park Café	Monsieur ('Mister')	8
Turkey	Grup Pan	Bana Bana ('To Me, To Me')	5
Iceland	Daníel Ágúst Haraldsson	það Sem Enginn Sér ('What No One Else Sees')	0

1990

Country	Artist	Song	Score
Italy	Toto Cutugno	Insieme 1992 ('Together 1992')	149
France	Joëlle Ursull	White And Black Blues	132
Ireland	Liam O'Reilly	Somewhere In Europe	132
Iceland	Stjórnin	Eittlagenn ('One More Song')	124
Spain	Azúcar Moreno	Bandido ('Bandit')	96
United Kingdom	Emma	Give A Little Love Back To The World	87
Yugoslavia	Tajči	Hajde Da Ludujemo ('Let's Go Crazy')	81
Denmark	Lonnie Devantier	Hallo Hallo ('Hello, Hello')	64
Germany	Chris Kempers & Daniel Kovac	Frei Zu Leben ('Free To Live')	60
Austria	Simone	Keine Mauern Mehr ('No Walls Anymore')	58
Switzerland	Egon Egemann	Musik Klingt In Die Welt Hinaus ('Music Sounds Around The World')	51
Belgium	Philippe Lafontaine	Macedomienne	46
Luxembourg	Céline Carzo	Quand Je Te Rêve ('When I Dream Of You')	38
Cyprus	Haris Anastazio	Milas Poli ('You Talk Too Much')	36
The Netherlands	Maywood	Ik Wil Alles Met Je Delen ('I Want To Share Everything With You')	25

APPENDIX 1

Country	Artist	Song	Score
Sweden	Edin Ådahl	Som En Vind ('Like A Wind')	24
Turkey	Kayahan	Gözlerinin Hapsindeyim ('Captive In Your Eyes')	21
Israel	Rita	Shara Ba-Rkhovot ('Singing In The Streets')	16
Greece	Christos Callow & Wave	Horis Skopo ('Without a Purpose')	11
Portugal	Nucha	Ha Sempre Alguem ('There's Always Someone')	9
Norway	Ketil Stokkan	Brandenburger Tor ('Brandenburg Gate')	8
Finland	Beat	Fri? ('Free?')	8

1991

Country	Artist	Song	Score
Sweden	Carola	Fångad Av En Stormvind ('Captured By A Stormwind')	146
France	Amina	C'Est Le Dernier Qui A Parlé Qui A Raison ('It's The Last One Who Spoke Who Is Right')	146
Israel	Duo Datz	Kan ('Here')	139
Spain	Sergio Dalma	Bailar Pegados ('Dancing Together')	119
Switzerland	Sandra Simó	Canzone Per Te ('A Song For You')	118
Malta	Georgina & Paul Giordimaina	Could It Be	106
Italy	Peppino Di Capri	Comme E Ddoce 'O Mare ('Like The Showers And The Sea')	89
Portugal	Dulce Pontes	Lusitana Paixão ('Lusitanian Passion')	62
Cyprus	Elena Patroklou	S.O.S.	60
Ireland	Kim Jackson	Could It Be That I'm In Love	47
United Kingdom	Samantha Janus	A Message To Your Heart	47
Turkey	Can Ugurlür, Izel Çeliköz & Reyhan Karaca	Iki Dakika ('Two Minutes')	44
Greece	Sophia Vossou	Anixi ('Spring')	36
Luxembourg	Sarah Bray	Un Baiser Volé ('A Stolen Kiss')	29

Country	Artist	Song	Score
Iceland	Stefán & Eyfi	Draumur Um Nina ('Dream About Nina')	26
Belgium	Clouseau	Geef Het Op ('Give It Up')	23
Norway	Just 4 Fun	Mrs Thompson	14
Germany	Atlantis 2000	Dieser Traum Darf Niemals Sterben ('This Dream Must Never Die')	10
Denmark	Anders Frandsen	Lige Der Hvor Hjertet Slår ('Right Where The Heart Is Beating')	8
Finland	Kaija	Hullu Yö ('Crazy Night')	6
Yugoslavia	Bebi Dol	Brazil	1
Austria	Thomas Forstner	Venedig In Regen ('Venice In The Rain')	0

1992

Country	Artist	Song	Score
Ireland	Linda Martin	Why Me	155
United Kingdom	Michael Ball	One Step Out Of Time	139
Malta	Mary Spiteri	Little Child	123
Italy	Mia Martini	Rapsodia ('Rhapsody')	111
Greece	Cleopatra	Olu Tu Kosmu I Elpitha ('All The Hope In The World')	94
Israel	Dafna	Ze Rak Sport ('It's Only sport')	85
Iceland	Heart 2 Heart	Nei Eða Já ('Yes Or No')	80
France	Kali	Monté La Rivie ('Climb The River')	73
The Netherlands	Humphrey Campbell	Wijs Me De Weg ('Show Me The Way')	67
Austria	Tony Wegas	Zusammen Geh'n ('Go Together')	63
Cyprus	Euridiki	Teria Zoume ('We Are Alike')	57
Denmark	Lotte Nilsson & Kenny Lübcke	Alt Det Som Ingen Ser ('What Nobody Sees')	47
Yugoslavia	Extra Nena	Ljubim Te Pesmama ('I'm Kissing You With Songs')	44
Spain	Serafin	Todo Esto Es La Musica ('All This Is Music')	37

Country	Artist	Song	Score
Switzerland	Daisy Auvray	Mister Music Man	32
Germany	Wind	Träume Sind Für Alle Da ('Dreams Are For Everbody')	27
Portugal	Dina	Amor D'Água Fresca ('Fresh Water Love')	26
Norway	Merethe Trøan	Visjoner ('Visions')	23
Turkey	Aylin Vatankoş	Yaz Bitti ('Summer Is Over')	17
Belgium	Morgane	Nous On Veut Des Violons ('We Want Violins')	11
Luxembourg	Marion Welter & Kontinent	Sou Fräi ('As Free')	10
Sweden	Christer Björkman	I Morgen Är En Annan Dag ('Tomorrow Is Another day')	9
Finland	Pave Maijanen	Yamma Yamma	4

1993

Country	Artist	Song	Score
Ireland	Niamh Kavanagh	In Your Eyes	187
United Kingdom	Sonia	Better The Devil You Know	164
Switzerland	Annie Cotton	Moi, Tout Simplement ('Quite Simply Me')	148
France	Patrick Fiori	Mama Corsica	121
Norway	Silje Vige	Alle Mine Tankar ('All My Thoughts')	120
The Netherlands	Ruth Jacott	Vrede ('Peace')	92
Sweden	Arvingarna	Eloise	89
Malta	William Mangion	This Time	69
Greece	Katherina Garbi	Ellanda, Hor A Tou Fotos ('Greece, Land Of Light')	64
Portugal	Anabela	A Cidade (Até Ser Dia) ('The City (Until Dawn)')	60
Spain	Eva Santamaria	Hombres ('Men')	58
Italy	Enrico Ruggeri	Sole D'Europa ('Sun Of Europe')	45
Iceland	Ingibjörg Stefánsdóttir	ψá Veistu Svarið ('Then You'll Know The Answer')	42
Austria	Tony Wegas	Maria Magdalena	32
Croatia	Put	Don't Ever Cry	31
Bosnia-Herzegovina	Muhamed Fazlagic	Sva Bol Svijeta ('All The Pain In The World')	27

Country	Artist	Song	Score
Finland	Katri-Helena	Tule Luo ('Come To Me')	20
Germany	Münchener Freiheit	Viel Zu Weit ('Much Too Far')	18
Cyprus	Zymboulokis & van Beke	Mi Stamatus ('Don't Stop')	17
Luxembourg	Modern Times	Donne-Moi Une Chance ('Give Me A Chance')	11
Turkey	Burak Aydos	Esmer Yarim ('My Darling Brunette')	10
Denmark	Tommy Seebach Band	Under Stjernerne På Himlen ('Under The Stars In The Sky')	9
Slovenia	1 x band	Tih Deževen Dan ('A Quiet Rainy Day')	9
Israel	Lahokat Shiru	Shiru ('Sing')	4
Belgium	Barbara	Iemand Als Jij ('Someone Like You')	3

1994

Country	Artist	Song	Score
Ireland	Paul Harrington & Charlie McGettigan	Rock'n'Roll Kids	226
Poland	Edyta Górniak	To Nie Ja ('That's Not Me')	166
Germany	Mekado	Wir Geben'Ne Party ('We're Giving A Party')	128
Hungary	Friderika Bayer	Kinek Mandjam El Vetkeimet ('To Whom Can I Confess My Sins')	122
Malta	Moira Stafrace & Christopher Scicluna	More Than Love	97
Norway	Elisabeth Andreassen & Jan Werner Danielsen	Duett ('Duet')	76
France	Nina Morato	Je Suis Un Vrai Garçon ('I'm A Tomboy')	74
Portugal	Sara Tavares	Chammar A Música ('Call The Music')	73
Russia	Youddiph	Vyechniy Stranik ('Eternal Wanderer')	70
United Kingdom	Frances Ruffelle	Lonely Symphony (We Will Be Free)	63
Cyprus	Evridiki	Ime Anthropos Ki Ego ('Im A Person Too')	51
Iceland	Sigga	Nætur ('Nights')	49

Country	Artist	Song	Score
Sweden	Marie Bergman & Roger Pontare	Stjärnorna ('Stars')	48
Greece	Kostas Bigalis	Diri, Diri (To Trehandiri) ('Diri, Diri (The Small Boat)')	44
Bosnia-Herzegovina	Alma & Dejan	Ostoni Kraj Mene ('Stay Beside Me')	39
Croatia	Tony Cetinski	Nek'ti Bude Ljubav Sva ('You May Have All The Love')	27
Austria	Petra Frey	Für Den Frieden Der Welt ('For The Peace Of The World')	19
Spain	Alejandro Abad	Ella No Es Ella ('She's Not Her')	17
Switzerland	Duilio	Sto Pregando ('I'm Praying')	15
Slovakia	Martin Durinda & Tublatanka	Nekonecná Piésen ('Never-Ending Song')	15
Romania	Dan Bittman	Dincolo De Nori ('Beyond The Clouds')	14
Finland	CatCat	Bye Bye Baby	11
The Netherlands	Willeke Alberti	Waar Is De Zon ('Where Is The Sun')	4
Estonia	Silvi Vrait	Nagu Merelaine ('Like A Seawave')	2
Lithuania	Ovidijus Vyšniauskas	Lopšiné Mylimai ('The Smell Of Your Lips Is Like Rain')	0

1995

Country	Artist	Song	Score
Norway	Secret Garden	Nocturne	148
Spain	Anabel Conde	Vuelve Conmigo ('Come Back to Me')	119
Sweden	Jan Johansen	Se På Mig ('Look At Me')	100
France	Nathalie Santamaria	Il Me Donne Rendez-vous ('He Makes A Rendezvous With Me')	94
Denmark	Aud Wilken	Fra Mols Til Skagen ('From Mols To Skagen')	92
Croatia	Magazin & Lidija	Nostalgija ('Nostalgia')	91
Slovenia	Darja Švajger	Prisluhni Mi ('Listen To Me')	84
Israel	Liora	Amen	81
Cyprus	Alexandros Panayi	Sti Fotia ('In The Fire')	79
United Kingdom	Love City Groove	Love City Groove	76
Malta	Mike Spiteri	Keep Me In Mind	76
Greece	Elina Konstantopoulou	Pia Prosefhi ('What Kind Of Prayer')	68
Austria	Stella Jones	Die Welt Dreht Sich Verkert ('The World Turns The Wrong Way')	67
Ireland	Eddie Friel	Dreamin'	44
Iceland	Bo Halldórsson	Nuna ('Now')	31

APPENDIX 1

Country	Artist	Song	Score
Turkey	Arzu Ece	Sev ('Love')	21
Russia	Philip Kirkorov	Kolybelnaya Dlya Vulkana ('Lullaby For A Volcano')	17
Poland	Justyna	Sama ('Alone')	15
Bosnia-Herzegovina	Davor Popović	Dvadeset Prvi Vijek ('The 21st Century')	14
Belgium	Frédéric Etherlinck	La Voix Est Libre ('The Voice Is Free')	8
Portugal	Tó Cruz	Baunilha E Chocolate ('Vanilla And Chocolate')	5
Hungary	Czaba Szigeti	Új Név Egy Régi Ház Falán ('A New Name On The Old House Wall')	3
Germany	Stone & Stone	Verliebt In Dich ('In Love With You')	1

1996

Country	Artist	Song	Score
Ireland	Eimear Quinn	The Voice	162
Norway	Elisabeth Andreassen	I Evighet ('For Eternity')	114
Sweden	One More Time	Den Vilda ('The Wild One')	100
Croatia	Maja Blagdan	Sveta Ljubav ('Holy Love')	98
Estonia	Maarja-Liis Ilus & Ivo Linna	Kaelakee Hääl ('Sound Of Necklace')	94
Portugal	Lucia Moniz	O Meu Coração Não Tem Cor ('My Heart Has No Colour')	92
The Netherlands	Maxine & Franklin Brown	De Eerste Keer ('The First Time')	78
United Kingdom	Gina G	Just A Little Bit	77
Cyprus	Constantinos	Mono Gia Mas ('Only For Us')	72
Malta	Miriam Christine	In A Woman's Heart	68
Austria	George Nussbaumer	Weils Da Guat Got ('Because You Feel Good')	68
Turkey	Şebnem Paker	Beşinci Mevsim ('The Fifth Season')	57
Iceland	Anna Mjöll	Sjúbídú ('Shooby-doo')	51
Greece	Mariana Efstratiou	Emis Forame To Himona Anixiatika ('We Wear Spring Clothes In Winter Time')	36

Country	Artist	Song	Score
Poland	Kasia Kowalska	Chcę Znać Swój Grzech ('I Want To Know My Sin')	31
Switzerland	Kathy Leander	Mon Cœur L'Aime ('My Heart Loves Him')	22
Belgium	Lisa del Bo	Liefde Is Een Kaartspel ('Life Is A Card Game')	22
Slovakia	Marcel Palonder	Kym Nas Mas ('Till You Have Us')	19
France	Dan Ar Braz & L'héritage Des Celtes	Diwanit Bugale ('May The Children Be Born')	18
Spain	Antonio Carbonelli	Ay, Que Deseo! ('Oh, What Desire!')	17
Slovenia	Regina	Dan Najlepših Sanj ('Day Of The Most Beautiful Dream')	16
Bosnia-Herzegovina	Amila Glamorcak	Za Našu Ijubav ('For Our Love')	13
Finland	Jasmine	Niin Kaunis On Taivas ('So Beautiful Is Heaven')	9

1997

Country	Artist	Song	Score
United Kingdom	Katrina & The Waves	Love Shine A Light	227
Ireland	Marc Roberts	Mysterious Woman	157
Turkey	Şebnem Paker & Grup Etnic	Dinle ('Listen')	121
Italy	Jalisse	Fiumi Di Parole ('Rivers Of Words')	114
Cyprus	Hara & Andreas Constantinou	Mana Mou ('Motherland')	98
Spain	Marcos Llunas	Sin Rencor ('Without Grudge')	96
France	Fanny	Sentiments, Songes ('Feelings, Dreams')	95
Estonia	Maarja Liis Ilus	Keelatud Maa ('Forbidden Land')	82
Malta	Debbie Scerri	Let Me Fly	66
Slovenia	Tanja Ribič	Zbudi Se ('Wake Up')	60
Poland	Anna-Maria Jopek	Ale Jestem ('But I Am')	54
Greece	Marianna Zorba	Horepse ('Dance')	39
Hungary	V.I.P.	Miért Kell, Hogy Elmenj? ('Why Do You Have To Go?')	39
Sweden	Blond	Bara Hon Älskar Mej ('If Only She Loves Me')	36
Russia	Alla Pugacheva	Primadonna	33
Denmark	Kølig Kaj	Stemmen I Mit Liv ('The Voice In My Life')	25

APPENDIX 1

Country	Artist	Song	Score
Croatia	ENI	Probudi Me ('Wake Me')	24
Bosnia-Herzegovina	Alma Čardžić	Goodbye	22
Germany	Bianca Shomburg	Zeit ('Time')	22
Iceland	Paul Oscar	Minn Hinsti Dans ('My Final Dance')	18
Austria	Bettina Soriat	One Step	12
Switzerland	Barbara Berta	Dentro Di Me ('Within Me')	5
The Netherlands	Mrs Einstein	Niemand Heeft Nog Tijd ('Nobody Has Time')	5
Norway	Tor Endresen	San Francisco	0
Portugal	Célia Lawson	Antes Do Adeus ('Before Goodbye')	0

1998

Country	Artist	Song	Score
Israel	Dana International	Diva	172
United Kingdom	Imaani	Where Are You?	166
Malta	Chiara	The One That I Love	165
The Netherlands	Edsilia Rombley	Hemel En Aarde ('Heaven And Earth')	150
Croatia	Danijela	Neka Mi Ne Svane ('May The Dawn Never Come')	131
Belgium	Mélanie Cohl	Dis Oui ('Say Yes')	122
Germany	Guildo Horn & The Orthopedic Stockings	Guildo Hat Euch Lieb ('Guildo Loves You')	86
Norway	Lars A. Fredriksen	Alltid Sommer ('Always Summer')	79
Ireland	Dawn	Is Always Over Now?	64
Sweden	Jill Johnson	Kärleken Är ('Love Is')	53
Cyprus	Michalis Hadjiyanni	Yenesis ('Genesis')	37
Estonia	Koit Toome	Mere Lapsed ('Children Of The Sea')	36
Portugal	Alma Lusa	Se Eu Te Pudesse Abraçar ('If Only I Could Embrace You')	36
Turkey	Tüzmen	Unutamazsin ('You Cannot Forget')	25
Finland	Edea	Aava ('Open Landscape')	22

Country	Artist	Song	Score
Spain	Mikel Herzog	Qué Voy A Hacer Sin Ti? ('What Will I Do Without You?')	21
Poland	Sixteen	To Takie Proste ('It's Easy')	19
Slovenia	Vili Resnik	Naj Bogovi Slišijo ('Let The Gods Hear')	17
FYR Macedonia	Vlado Janevski	Ne Zori, Zoro ('Dawn, Do Not Rise')	16
Greece	Thalassa	Mia Krifi Evesthisia ('A Secret Illusion')	12
Slovakia	Katerína Hasprová	Modlitba ('A Prayer')	8
Romania	Mālina Olinescu	Eu Cred ('I Believe')	6
Hungary	Charlie	A Holnap Már Nem Lesz Szomorú ('Sadness Will Be Over Tomorrow')	4
France	Marie Line	Où Aller ('Where To Go')	3
Switzerland	Gunvor Guggisberg	Lass 'Ihn ('Let Him')	0

1999

Country	Artist	Song	Score
Sweden	Charlotte Nilsson	Take Me To Your Heaven	163
Iceland	Selma Björnsdóttir	All Out Of Luck	146
Germany	Sürpriz	Reise Nach Jerusalem ('Journey To Jerusalem')	140
Croatia	Doris Dragovic	Marija Magdalena ('Mary Magdalene')	118
Israel	Eden	Yom Huledet ('Happy Birthday')	93
Estonia	Evelin Samuel & Camille	Diamond Of Night	90
Bosnia-Herzegovina	Dino & Beatrice	Putnici	86
Denmark	Trine Jepsen & Michael Teschl	This Time I Mean It	71
The Netherlands	Marlayne	One Good Reason	71
Austria	Bobbie Singer	Reflection	65
Slovenia	Darja Svaiger	For A Thousand Years	50
Belgium	Venessa Chinitor	Like The Wind	38
United Kingdom	Precious	Say It Again	38
Norway	Stig Van Eijk	Living My Life Without You	35
Malta	Times 3	Believe In Peace	32
Turkey	Tuba Önal & Grup Mistik	Dön Artik ('Come Back')	21
Ireland	Karen & Bronagh Mullan	When You Need Me	18

Country	Artist	Song	Score
Poland	Mieczieslaw Szcześniak	Przytul Mnie Mocno ('Hold Me Tight')	17
France	Nayah	Je Veux Donner Ma Voix ('I Want To Give My Voice')	14
Lithuania	Aiste Smilgeviciute	Strazdas ('The Song Thrush')	13
Portugal	Rui Bandeira	Como Tudo Começou ('How Everything Began')	12
Cyprus	Marlain Angelidou	Tha 'Nai Erotas ('It Will Be Love')	2
Spain	Lydia	No Quiero Escuchar ('I Don't Want To Listen')	1

2000

Country	Artist	Song	Score
Denmark	The Olsen Brothers	Fly On The Wings Of Love	195
Russia	Alsou	Solo	155
Latvia	Brainstorm	My Star	136
Estonia	Ines	Once In A Lifetime	98
Germany	Stefan Raab	Wadde Hadde Dudde Aa? ('What Do You Have There?')	96
Ireland	Eamonn Toal	Millennium Of Love	92
Sweden	Roger Pontare	When Spirits Are Calling My Name	88
Malta	Claudette Pace	Desire	73
Croatia	Goran Karan	Kada Zaspu Anđeli (Ostani) ('When Angels Fall Asleep (Stay)')	70
Turkey	Pinar Ayhan & The SOS	Yorgunum Anla ('Understand That I'm Weary')	59
Norway	Charmed	My Heart Goes Boom	57
Iceland	Telma & Ágúst	Tell Me	45
The Netherlands	Linda Wagenmakers	No Goodbyes	40
Austria	The Rounder Girls	All To You	34
FYR Macedonia	XXL	100% Te Ljubam ('I Love You 100%')	29
United Kingdom	Nicki French	Don't Play That Song Again	28

APPENDIX 1

Country	Artist	Song	Score
Romania	Taxi	The Moon	25
Spain	Serafin Zubiri	Colgado De Un Sueño ('Hanging Onto A Dream')	18
Finland	Nina Åström	A Little Bit	18
Switzerland	Jane Bogaert	La Vita Cosé? ('What Is Life?')	14
Cyprus	Voice	Nomiza ('I Believed')	8
Israel	Ping Pong	Sameach ('All Happy')	7
France	Sofia Mestari	On Aura Le Ciel ('We'll Have The Sky')	5
Belgium	Nathalie Sorce	L'Envie De Vivre ('The Wish To Live')	2

2001

Country	Artist	Song	Score
Estonia	Tanel Padar, Dave Benton & 2XL	Everybody	198
Denmark	Rollo & King	Never Ever Let You Go	177
Greece	Antique	Die For You	147
France	Natasha St-Pier	Ja N'ai Que Mon Âme ('I Only Have My Soul')	142
Sweden	Friends	Listen To Your Heartbeat	100
Spain	David Civera	Dile Que La Quiero ('Tell Her That I Love Her')	76
Slovenia	Nuša Derenda	Energy	70
Germany	Michelle	Wer Liebe Lebt ('If You Live Love')	66
Malta	Fabrizio Faniello	Another Summer Night	48
Croatia	Vanna	Strings Of My Heart	42
Turkey	Sedat Yüce	Sevgiliye Son ('The End Of Love')	41
Russia	Mumiy Troll	Lady Alpine Blue	37
Lithuania	Skamp	You Got Style	35
Bosnia-Herzegovina	Nino Pršeš	Hano ('Hannah')	29
United Kingdom	Lindsay Dracass	No Dream Impossible	28
Israel	Tal Sundak	'En Davar ('Never Mind')	25
Portugal	MTM	Eu Só Sei Ser Feliz Assim ('I Only Can Be Happy This Way')	18

Country	Artist	Song	Score
Latvia	Arnis Mednis	Too Much	16
The Netherlands	Michelle	Out On My Own	16
Poland	Piasek	2 Long	11
Ireland	Gary O'Shaughnessy	Without Your Love	6
Iceland	Two Tricky	Angel	3
Norway	Haldor Lægreid	On My Own	3

2002

Country	Artist	Song	Score
Latvia	Marie N.	I Wanna	176
Malta	Ira Losco	7th Wonder	164
Estonia	Sahlene	Runaway	111
United Kingdom	Jessica Garlick	Come Back	111
France	Sandrine François	Il Faut Du Temps ('It Takes Time')	104
Cyprus	One	Gimme	85
Spain	Rosa	Europe's Living A Celebration	81
Sweden	Afro-dite	Never Let It Go	72
Romania	Monica Anghel & Marcel Pavel	Tell Me Why	71
Russia	Premier Ministr	Northern Girl	55
Croatia	Vesna Pisarović	Everything I Want	44
Israel	Sarit Hadad	Light A Candle	37
Belgium	Sergio & The Ladies	Sister	33
Slovenia	Sestre	Samo Ljubezen ('Only Love')	33
Bosnia-Herzegovina	Maja Tatić	Na Jastuka Za Dvoje ('On A Pillow For Two')	33
Turkey	Buket Bengisu & Group Sapphire	Leylaklar Soldu Kalbinde ('The Lilacs Faded In Your Heart')	29
Greece	Michalis Rakintzis	S.A.G.A.P.O. ('I.L.O.V.E.U.')	27
Austria	Manuel Ortega	Say A Word	26

Country	Artist	Song	Score
FYR Macedonia	Karolina	Od Nas Zavisi ('It's Up To Us')	25
Finland	Laura Voutilainen	Addicted To You	24
Germany	Corinna May	I Can't Live Without Music	17
Switzerland	Francine Jordi	Dans Le Jardin De Mon Âme ('In The Garden Of My Soul')	15
Lithuania	Aivaras	Happy You	12
Denmark	Malene Mortensen	Tell Me Who You Are	7

2003

Country	Artist	Song	Score
Turkey	Sertab Erener	Everyway That I Can	167
Belgium	Urban Trad	Sanomi	165
Russia	t.A.T.u.	Ne Ver', Ne Bojsia ('Don't Believe, Don't Be Afraid')	164
Norway	Jostein Hasselgård	I'm Not Afraid To Move On	123
Sweden	Fame	Give Me Your Love	107
Austria	Alf Poier	Weil Der Mensch Zählt ('Man Is The Measure Of All Things')	101
Poland	Ich Troje	Keine Grenzen ('No Borders')	90
Spain	Beth	Dime ('Tell Me')	81
Iceland	Birgitta	Open Your Heart	81
Romania	Nicola	Don't Break My Heart	73
Ireland	Mickey Harte	We've Got The World Tonight	53
Germany	Lou	Let's Get Happy	53
The Netherlands	Esther Hart	One More Night	45
Ukraine	Olexandr	Hasta La Vista	30
Croatia	Claudia Beni	Vise Nisam Tvoja ('I Can't Be Your Lover')	29
Bosnia-Herzegovina	Mija Martina	Ne Brini ('Could It Be')	27
Greece	Mando	Never Let You Go	25

Country	Artist	Song	Score
France	Louisa Baileche	Monts Et Merveilles ('The Moon And The Stars')	19
Israel	Lior Narkis	Words For Love	17
Cyprus	Stelios Konstantas	Feeling Alive	15
Estonia	Ruffus	Eighties Coming Back	14
Portugal	Rita Guerra	Deixa-Me Sonhar ('Keep The Dream Alive')	13
Slovenia	Karmen	Nanana	7
Latvia	F.L.Y.	Hello From Mars	5
Malta	Lynn Chircop	To Dream Again	4
United Kingdom	Jemini	Cry Baby	0

APPENDIX 2

Silliest song titles in Eurovision

(So far, that is!)

Voi Voi	(Norway, 1960)
Ring-Dinge-Ding	(The Netherlands, 1967)
Boum Badaboum	(Monaco, 1967)
La, La, La	(Spain, 1968)
Boom Bang-a-Bang	(The United Kingdom, 1969)
Tom Tom Tom	(Finland, 1973)
Ding-Dinge-Dong	(The Netherlands, 1975)
Pump Pump	(Finland, 1976)
Boom Boom Boomerang	(Austria, 1977)
Dai-Li-Dou	(Portugal, 1978)
Boom Boom	(Denmark, 1978)
A-Ba-Ni-Bi	(Israel, 1978)
Hey, Na Na	(Belgium, 1979)
Humanahum	(France, 1981)
Bem Bom	(Portugal, 1982)
Diggi-loo, Diggi-ley	(Sweden, 1984)
Didai Didai Dai	(Turkey, 1985)
Bana Bana	(Turkey, 1989)
Yamma Yamma	(Finland, 1992)
Diri, Diri	(Greece, 1994)

APPENDIX 3

'Let's go to the Scoreboard'

The following is a list of all the countries who have ever won an ESC and the number of times they have won:

Country	No. of Times	Years
Ireland	7	(1970, 1980, 1987, 1992, 1993, 1994, 1996)
France	5	(1958, 1960, 1962, 1969, 1977)
Luxembourg	5	(1961, 1965, 1972, 1973, 1983)
United Kingdom	5	(1967, 1969, 1976, 1981, 1997)
Sweden	4	(1974, 1984, 1991, 1999)
The Netherlands	4	(1957, 1959, 1969, 1975)
Israel	3	(1978, 1979, 1998)
Denmark	2	(1963, 2000)
Italy	2	(1964, 1990)
Norway	2	(1985, 1995)
Spain	2	(1968, 1969)
Switzerland	2	(1956, 1988)
Austria	1	(1966)
Belgium	1	(1986)
Estonia	1	(2001)
Germany	1	(1982)
Latvia	1	(2002)
Monaco	1	(1971)
Turkey	1	(2003)
Yugoslavia	1	(1989)

APPENDIX 4

'nul points'

Country	Year	Song	Artist
Norway	1963	Solhverv	Anita Thallaug
	1978	Mil Etter Mil	Jahn Teigen
	1981	Aldri I Livet	Finn Kalvik
	1997	San Francisco	Tor Endresen
Austria	1962	Nur In Der Wiener Luft	Eleonore Schwarz
	1988	Lisa, Mona Lisa	Wilfried
	1991	Venedig In Regen	Thomas Forstner
Finland	1963	Muistojeni Laulu	Laila Halme
	1965	Aurinko Laskee Länteen	Viktor Klimenko
	1982	Nuku Pommiin	Kojo
Spain	1962	Llamame	Victor Balaguer
	1965	Qué Bueno, Qué Bueno	Conchita Bautista
	1983	Quién Maneja Mi Barca?	Remedios Amaya
Switzerland	1964	I Miei Pensieri	Anita Traversi
	1967	Quel Cœur Vas-Tu Briser?	Geraldine
	1998	Lass'Ihn	Gunvor Guggisberg
Belgium	1962	Ton Num	Fud Leclerc
	1965	Als Het Weer Lente Is	Lize Marke
Germany	1964	Men Gewöhnt Sich....	Nora Nova
	1965	Paradies, Wo Bist Du?	Ulla Wiesner
The Netherlands	1962	Katinka	De Spelbrekers
	1963	Een Speeldoos	Annie Palmen

Country	Year	Song	Artist
Portugal	1964	Oração	António Calvário
	1997	Antes Do Adeus	Célia Lawson
Turkey	1983	Opera	Cetin Alp & the Short Waves
	1987	Şarkim Sevgi Üstüne	Seyyal Taner & Locomotif
Iceland	1989	það Sem Enginn Sér	Daníel Ágúst Haraldsson
Italy	1966	Dio Come Ti Amo	Domenico Modugno
Lithuania	1994	Lopšiné Mylimai	Ovidijus Vyšniauskas
Luxembourg	1970	Je Suis Tombé Du Ciel	David Alexander Winter
Monaco	1966	Bien Plus Fort	Tereza
Sweden	1963	En Gång I Stockholm	Monica Zetterlund
United Kingdom	2003	Cry Baby	Jemini
Yugoslavia	1964	Život Je Sklopio Krug	Sabahudin Kurt

APPENDIX 5

2004 Score Sheets

Eurovision Song Contest Qualifying Round 2004

This is the semi-final to be held in Istanbul in May 2004. The top ten songs from this round will go into the final of the Eurovision Song Contest.

Either fill in the scores or run your own sweep at your Eurovision party.

Country	Artist	Song	Score
Albania			
Andorra			
Belarus			
Bosnia-Herzegovina			
Croatia			
Cyprus			
Denmark			
Estonia			
Finland			
FYR Macedonia			
Greece			
Israel			
Latvia			
Lithuania			
Malta			
Monaco			
The Netherlands			
Portugal			
Serbia & Montenegro			
Slovenia			
Switzerland			
Ukraine			

Eurovision Song Contest Final 2004

The top ten countries from the 2003 contest automatically qualified for the main event (along with the Big Four) and are listed below. Remember to add the top ten who win the Qualifying Round to make up the 24 entries.

Country Score	Artist	Song
Austria		
Belgium		
France		
Germany		
Iceland		
Ireland		
Norway		
Poland		
Romania		
Russia		
Spain		
Sweden		
Turkey		
United Kingdom		

Recommended Websites

http://esctoday.com/
This is the official Eurovision website where you can get all the latest
ESC news and have your say in the online forum. You can also
submit your song or lyrics in the Songwriters Contest (international
entries accepted!).

http://www.eurovision.tv/ebu/micro_index.htm
The official site for the 2004 contest in Instanbul.

http://diggiloo.net/
Great for English translations of all your favourite Eurovision songs.

http://eurovisionsongcontest.start4all.com/
Great links to Eurovision websites such as fanclubs and newsletters
as well as official sites.

http://eurovisionarchive.cjb.net/
Not just an archive, you can also send Eurovision greeting cards and
download screensavers and ring tones for your mobile phone.

http://www.eurovisionhouse.nl/index2.htm
'The House of Eurovision' is constantly updated if you're keen to be
part of the build up to the next song contest. You can also check out
the winner of the Barbara Dex Award for the worst-dressed artist in
the contest for the year (voting opens the day after the final).

http://www.cowgate.demon.co.uk/mit/drinking/eurovision.html
A must for every Eurovision party – the Eurovision Drinking Game.
Suggestions are accepted so, start watching Eurovision and write to
these guys.

http://eurovision.xeeu.com/
Incredibly comprehensive site, it will come up as Ron's Eurovision
Page.

RECOMMENDED WEBSITES

http://www.geocities.com/jamoismac/
This site comes up as Whoops Dragovic and is one of the funnier sites on the net about Eurovision.

http://geocities.com/national_finals/
This is a fantastic site if you want to learn more about the National Finals of each individual country going right back to 1956. They'll even email you to let you know when the site has been updated.

http://eurosong.net/
A Eurovision song database listed by year, by country and by winners, with its own search engine. You can also chat in real-time, leave messages and post your opinions on anything related to Eurovision.

http://www.eurosong.net/songthrush/
For the lyrics of every song performed at Eurovision since 1956, including different language versions for those of you who like a bit of a challenge.

Acknowledgements

Thanks to John Stahel and Rod Webb for starting it all and to Margaret Meehan for making it work.

Thanks also to Jody Lee. Every first timer should have an editor as great as her and special thanks to the Belgian entry, Jeanne Ryckmans, for having the idea in the first place.

About the Author

Des Mangan has been writing comedy for nearly twenty years and vows to keep going till he gets it right. In the late eighties he created the popular live show 'Double Take', which toured Australia, England and a little place in Ireland that he has forgotten the name of. From this show came the 1993 film *Hercules Returns*, which he also wrote and voiced. He is currently bribing a large company to release it on DVD.

He was Head Writer for eight years on the highly successful Sydney radio show Wendy Harmer and the 2DAYFM Morning Crew and, at the same time, hosted the Cult Movie on SBS on Saturday nights while balancing a large stack of plates on his head. He is also the commentator for the Eurovision Song Contest seen annually on SBS.

Des is currently working on two film scripts, a television comedy and a particularly difficult jigsaw puzzle.